HEROES of AMERICA™

Babe RUTH

by **Len Canter**

illustrations by **Pablo Marcos**

BARONET
B·O·O·K·S

BARONET BOOKS, New York, New York

HEROES OF AMERICA™

Edited by
Joshua Hanft and Rochelle Larkin

HEROES OF AMERICA™ is a series of dramatized lives of great Americans especially written for younger readers. We have selected men and women whose accomplishments and achievements can inspire children to set high goals for themselves and work with all of us for a better tomorrow.

Table of Contents

Important Dates

1895 George (Babe) Ruth born in Baltimore, Maryland

1914 Babe signs with minor league team, Baltimore Orioles

1914 Babe called up to the majors, signs with Boston Red Sox

1915 Babe hits first major-league home run

1916 Babe wins first World Series pitching victory with Red Sox

1917 Babe wins career-high 24 games

1918 Babe's record setting $29\frac{2}{3}$ innings streak of scoreless World Series pitching ends

1920 Babe Ruth sold to New York Yankees

1921 Babe sets new career-high single season home run record with 59

1927 Babe breaks his own record with 60 home runs

1929 Babe hits 500th career home run

1933 Babe homers in first All-Star game ever played

1934 Babe hits 700th career home run

1935 Babe joins Boston Braves as player-assistant manager and retires at end of season

1948 Babe's final appearance at Yankee Stadium

1948 Babe Ruth dies of cancer at age 53

Chapter 1

Baltimore's Bad Boy

George was holding back the tears, trying to look brave. A policeman had a firm grip on the seven-year-old boy as he pulled him along the cobblestone streets in the ramshackle waterfront section of 1902 Baltimore, Maryland.

"George Ruth, I've looked the other way before," scolded the officer, "but this time we're going to have a little talk with your father." George didn't even look up as they arrived at the somber row house on West Camden Street. Two railroad men, walking

"Isn't That Little George with the Law?"

arm in arm, burst out into the street from the saloon that was owned by the Ruth family. They were dirty and smelled of the sea.

"Hey! Isn't that little George with the law?" one man exclaimed. "What did you do, kid, steal an apple or break a window?" The men laughed. "Be on your way before you get the same. My business is with Mr. Ruth, not with the likes of you." The officer tapped his nightstick. The smiles vanished from the men's faces, and they quickly shuffled down the block.

George's family lived above the bar that his dad tended. The Ruths worked long, hard hours, as the saloon was open all day and most of the night. Grizzled longshoremen, who worked all night loading ships in the harbor, and merchant marines just back from long ocean voyages came in and out at all hours to drink, gamble, and swap stories about their adventures.

George was no stranger to the regular customers who watched him play under the barstools on the sawdust-covered floor. Out of his father's sight, the customers would sometimes slip George a puff of a cigar and then roar with laughter. Big George, as Mr. Ruth was known, was too busy working to notice these pranks that so delighted the crowd.

When George was only five years old, he began to slip out and roam the streets. Before long he had met most of the toughest kids along the waterfront, living the life of the streets, fighting and sometimes even stealing. By the time he was seven, he had been in more trouble than most kids could ever imagine.

The gang George ran with learned always to keep one step ahead of the local police. One of their favorite antics was to steal some fruit from an outdoor stand, throw it at an unsuspecting wagon

The Gang George Ran With

driver, and then to run and hide, laughing as the police tried to find them. Sometimes the boys wandered down to a large vacant lot where they watched men playing baseball, a game that had become very popular just about everywhere. When the lot was vacant they themselves would play, using a stick for a bat and rolled-up socks with a rock in the middle for a ball.

George's parents begged him to attend school. In fact, it was on this very warm spring day that his father had instructed George to spend the day at school "or else." Instead George went to meet his friends who were busy throwing rocks at the locomotives over at the Camden Rail yard. A window had been broken and before he could get away, George was grabbed by a rail-yard policeman who held on to him all the way home.

As the policeman and George entered the smoky tavern, the music and laughter stopped. The police were not a welcome sight here, and the elder Ruth scowled from behind the bar.

"It's a little more serious this time, Mr. Ruth," the officer explained. "The boys broke some windows and damaged some railroad property. I'm afraid that if you and your wife can't handle the boy, I'll have to recommend that he be placed in a reformatory. The boy's up to no good, Mr. Ruth. He's headed for a life of trouble."

After glancing around suspiciously at the hushed onlookers, the officer went back out. Conversation began again among the customers. George anxiously waited for his father to speak.

"George, go upstairs until I can attend to you," his father said.

George hurried upstairs. He wondered what kind of punishment awaited him and grew more nervous as he imagined his fate. A few hours had gone by when he heard footsteps coming up

Big George Looked Angry.

the stairs.

When the door swung open, he saw his father and his mother, who was holding his baby sister, Mamie. His mother had tears running down her cheeks. Big George looked as angry as the boy had ever seen him. He walked toward George with an angry scowl, but stopped a few feet short of where George sat. His face returned to normal as he spoke to his son in a quiet and deliberate voice.

"George," his father began, "you have made a lot of problems for our family. Tomorrow I am taking you to a place where they might be able to straighten you out, give you some education, and teach you how to become a good man."

George had no idea where such a place could be or even what his father was talking about. Suddenly there was a crash of broken glass downstairs. Mr. Ruth hurried down to the bar. Mrs. Ruth followed, stopping once to look at her son. Only two of her eight children had survived their hard life and, despite all the problems George had caused, it was hard for her to say good-bye to her only son.

George was awakened very early the next morning. His mother, looking tired and drawn, brought in some clean clothes for him to wear. She had packed a little bag for him. Without saying a word, his father led him down the street to the trolley station. They took a ride to a part of the city that George had never seen before. In fact, George had never really been away from the few blocks around the tavern.

This other section of Baltimore was very different than the waterfront. The sky was blue and the air here was clear and didn't smell from fish and smoke. There were trees and finely-dressed people window-shopping.

They walked up to a big red brick building surrounded by a high iron fence with a great black gate.

A Big Red Building

After a pause, George's father took a deep breath and said, "George, this is St. Mary's, and you will be staying here from now on." With that he grabbed his son's hand and led him through the gate.

St. Mary's Industrial School for Boys was home to children from many different backgrounds. It was not just a reform school for bad, "incorrigible" boys as George was thought to be. St. Mary's was also an orphanage and took in boys from very poor families that could not afford to take care of them. There were hundreds of boys living at St. Mary's, and on this day George Herman Ruth became one of the youngest among them.

Chapter 2

Life at St. Mary's

While George and his father waited for someone to greet them, George had a little time to think about the situation he had gotten himself into. He didn't much like the looks of the place with its iron gates. But he was sure that he was tough enough to take care of himself there. Besides, he figured he would be out and back with his friends in no time. The boy hadn't lost any of his cocky confidence; only his freedom

St. Mary's was run by the Xaverian Brothers, a

The Brother Began to Explain the Rules.

Catholic order. One of the Brothers called out to the Ruths to enter the inner office. When they were settled, the Brother began to explain the rules by which all the boys at St. Mary's had to live. He was a kindly man who spoke softly and used big words that George had not heard before. He quickly made it clear, however, that discipline was strict and that punishments were severe.

All the boys had to attend class every day and also receive training in a trade, learning a skill they could work at when they were grown men. To George, this all sounded like the worst punishment he could ever imagine! He wasn't even sure what "living by the rules" really meant since he had never done so before.

George remained seated, staring at the Brother while the man filled out some papers, all the while wondering what could possibly happen next.

When he finished his paperwork, the Brother

turned to George, and with a smile said, "Come, let us go and meet your new friends."

In St. Mary's main building, they entered a huge room lined with rows of beds on one side, all neatly made up and all exactly the same. On another wall was a group of lockers. The Brother explained that this was George's new home, where he would sleep and wash and where he would keep his things.

George was led to a bed on the end, where he was surprised to see a new blanket and pillow which were to be his and his alone! And he was given his own locker in which he saw some pencils and paper.

Suddenly a bell rang. The doors to the big room flew open and a hundred boys noisily pushed and shoved their way inside. As the boys settled on their cots or fiddled with their lockers, the Brother told George that these were the boys he would eat, sleep, and go to school with, and that if he'd "make the

A Hundred Boys Pushed Noisily.

best of it and stay out of trouble, then he would be very happy at St. Mary's."

As soon as the Brother left the room, a few of the older boys walked over and surrounded George. George looked them over. They stared back just as hard.

"Hey, kid, where'd you come from?" demanded the biggest.

"What's it your business?" George snapped back.

The boys looked each other over from head to toe. Many of the faces George saw reminded him of his pals on the waterfront. Many of the kids surrounding him were from poor families, just as he was.

Some had even run away from home and been picked up by the police in Baltimore; George even thought that he recognized an older boy from his neighborhood, one he thought had landed in jail.

Others were orphans, but the one thing they all had in common was that they had been sent to St. Mary's to live until they turned 21.

George stood up defiantly, waiting for someone to start something, but no one did. With his mean scowl, George looked so fierce that the others figured he must be just like them, and would make a better friend than enemy.

The morning wake up call came very early. It was not even light out yet and the big room was cold. The routine at St. Mary's was unlike anything George had ever experienced. After waking at six A.M., the "inmates," as they liked to call themselves, quickly dressed, attended church, and then walked single file to breakfast.

This ritual was all very peculiar to George, but he had to admit that the breakfast was about the best he had ever had. Still, he itched to be able to walk through the gate and go home. But one glance

He Could Neither Read Nor Write.

outside the window at the high iron fence reminded him that he was there to stay.

Then it was on to the schoolroom. Except for lunchtime and recess, the boys attended school and workshops all day. The Brother who taught the class came in and passed out some books. Each boy was expected to take a turn reading aloud.

When it was George's turn, his face flushed red and he sputtered; he could neither read nor write at all. After all, he had spent most of his boyhood figuring out ways to avoid going to school!

After a moment of snickering from some of his older classmates, George admitted to the Brother that he couldn't read. Then he boldly said, "If the other kids learned to read, so can I." He started learning that very day.

At recess that afternoon, a fight started between two of the older boys involved in a game of kickball. Others joined in and soon the yard was filled with fighting children. George watched excitedly as the two teens punched wildly at each other.

Suddenly a huge, lone figure dressed in a Brother's robe came toward them. Without any words from the man, the fight immediately stopped and the boys dusted themselves off. The game restarted and everything went back to normal.

George wondered aloud, "Who was that guy, a cop or something?"

Another boy answered, "That's Brother Matthias and you'd better watch out for him, pal. When you get out of line around here, he's the one who's gonna give it to you."

Later that day Brother Matthias came to the dorm to introduce himself to George. He was in charge of keeping the boys in line at St. Mary's, and many of the younger kids were afraid of crossing him. But the boys also knew that Brother Matthias was always fair in handing out any discipline.

Keeping the Boys in Line

BABE RUTH

He was a big man, well over six feet tall and close to 250 pounds, a giant compared to the seven-year-old George Ruth. The boys at St. Mary's were all impressed with the Brother's size and strength, but somehow he looked strict and friendly at the same time. Most of the boys admired and even loved him.

As for George, he took an instant liking to Brother Matthias. Despite the young Ruth's reputation as a bad apple, Brother Matthias found George easy to like, too. He gave him more attention than George had ever gotten from his own parents back at the saloon.

George soon found out something else about Brother Matthias: he was in charge of many of the school's sports teams, including the baseball team.

Chapter 3

Play Ball!

It didn't take long for George to settle into life at St. Mary's. He eventually chose to work in the school's tailor shop, and he became quite good at putting collars on shirts. All the boys who worked in the shop were paid a few cents for each shirt they completed. They were allowed to use the money they earned to buy candy at a little store that was part of St. Mary's.

Often George put aside his tough guy act long enough to share his candy with younger, smaller

Real Bats and Balls

boys who had just come to St. Mary's and who felt as lonely and scared as he had at first.

When spring came around, Brother Matthias invited George to join one of St. Mary's baseball teams. It seemed like everybody in the school was talking about the upcoming baseball season. Many of the boys begged Brother Matthias to tell them the same stories they had heard last year, tales about already legendary players like Christy Mathewson, Honus Wagner and Ty Cobb.

Although George hadn't played much baseball before he entered St. Mary's, he took to the game right away. He developed a keen batting eye and smooth pitching motion by playing a special game the boys called "Pokenins." One player batted until the pitcher got him out; then they switched positions. Best of all, instead of the sticks and rocks the boys along the waterfront had to use, the teams at St. Mary's got to play with real bats and balls, and even had leather gloves to catch with.

George practiced under the watchful eye of Brother Matthias. Recognizing George's ability right away, Brother Matthias often spent hours hitting his pupil grounder after grounder. Each year he spent at St. Mary's, George became a better player. After trying a number of positions around the diamond, he decided that his favorite was catcher.

The problem was that George was left-handed and the school only owned right-handed catcher's mitts. George had to wear the mitt on his left hand, his throwing hand. As soon as he caught the ball he would drop the glove, move the ball to his left hand and then throw. Despite this, George became the best catcher at St. Mary's.

Brother Matthias soon put him on a team with boys who were three or four years older than he was. George learned to use the mitt on either hand and even started to play a little at third base,

Grounder After Grounder

another unusual baseball position for a left-hander. He had speed and he could hit, smashing extra-base hits to all fields.

One day George's team was having a really bad day. The starting pitcher couldn't seem to get any-one out, and neither could his replacement. George began to snicker, poking fun at his teammates' inability to throw strikes. Suddenly time was called and Brother Matthias rushed out onto the field.

"What are you laughing at, Ruth?" he demanded to know.

George couldn't help himself and continued to giggle as Brother Matthias glared at him, waiting for an answer.

"I'm sorry, Coach," George finally stammered, "but these boys are about as sorry an excuse for pitchers as I've ever seen. It struck me as kind of funny."

Brother Matthias fumed as he stood next to

George. "All right, Mr. Ruth, let's see what you can do," he said, tossing George the ball.

"Me?" asked George, a frown replacing his smile. "Coach, you know I've never pitched before. I don't know how to pitch! Don't put me in there now."

"Oh, but you know enough to say that your buddies can't get the job done," said the Brother. "Now get out there and show everyone the way it's supposed to be done!"

George didn't even know exactly how to stand on the mound. Everybody was staring at him, waiting for something to happen. The umpire yelled, "Play ball!" and the batter stepped up.

George toed the rubber, and with all his strength fired a fastball down the middle for a strike. Not so bad, George thought, and then did it again. Then, much to his astonishment, he flipped a nasty little curve ball. The batter missed by a mile and struck out. By the next inning, George found

More Enjoyable than Catching

himself in a real pitching groove. Even Brother Matthias, who had only hoped to teach George another kind of lesson, was smiling as he stood in a corner of the dugout.

After his fourth inning of shutout work, George came off the field grinning, this time because he realized that he had found something even more enjoyable than catching. For the rest of the season George pitched, caught a few games, and displayed lots of ability at the plate. In just a few years, George Herman Ruth became one of the best players at St. Mary's.

Of course, during his time at St. Mary's George did more than just play baseball. He learned to read and write and to respect the other kids. The concentration needed to be a good pitcher, and having to handle the pressures of a big game, taught him how to control himself a little better.

When Brother Matthias formed St. Mary's All-

Stars, a team that played road games outside the school, he chose George as one of his pitchers.

In every baseball game he played, it seemed that George did something spectacular either in the field or at the plate. The Baltimore newspapers, hungry for any baseball news for their readers, often covered these All-Star games, and the list of the young star's exploits increased with every year.

His reputation on the baseball diamond grew nearly as fast as his size. George was no longer a scruffy little boy. As a teenager he stood six-feet-two and was a strong, hard 180 pounds.

During George's last year at St. Mary's, it was usual for him to hit a home run in every game. When he pitched he was nearly unhittable, staying undefeated for the entire season. Professional baseball men were beginning to take notice of the hard-hitting, strong-armed young man. And soon

No Longer a Scruffy Little Boy

something happened that would change George Ruth's life forever.

At that time, minor league baseball was very important. It was the only place prospects had a chance to play baseball every day and possibly become good enough to catch on with one of the sixteen Major League teams.

The great teams of the era, like the New York Giants and the Philadelphia Athletics, got most of their new players from these minor league teams whose owners made a lot of money by finding, developing and then selling the players.

Jack Dunn was one of the minor-league owners. A gruff former player, he owned and managed the Baltimore Orioles, then a team with a great tradition in the International League. Dunn was always on the lookout for good young players. Like everyone else in Baltimore, he had read about young George Ruth.

BABE RUTH

One cold, snowy February day in 1914, about a week after George's nineteenth birthday, he got a note in class to see Brother Matthias. When he walked in, another man was there to greet him.

"Hiya, kid, I'm Jack Dunn, manager of the Baltimore Orioles. I'll get right to the point, George. Brother Matthias tells me that you can throw a baseball pretty hard. How would you like to pitch for the Orioles?"

George was stunned. Although he was the star player at St. Mary's, he had never even dreamed of becoming a pro. He figured that after his time at St. Mary's he would become a tailor just as he had been trained to do. Now he stood with his mouth wide open, searching for the words to answer Mr. Dunn.

"Well, boy, what do you think?" Dunn asked. "We've got a swell bunch of fellas on the team and I think you could start playing almost right away!"

Finally George blurted out, "Well, sir, I guess

"Pay Me . . . to Play?"

playing ball would be a lot more fun than making shirts!"

Dunn smiled and asked, "How about six hundred to start?"

George didn't understand what Mr. Dunn meant. He was speechless.

"George," said Brother Matthias, "it's not like you not to have something to say on a subject. Mr. Dunn has just offered you six hundred dollars a year to play baseball. What do you think of that?"

"You mean you'd . . . pay me . . . to play?" George stammered, shaking his head in disbelief.

"Of course we'll have to turn guardianship over to you," Brother Matthias was now saying to Mr. Dunn. "When do you need him?"

With George daydreaming about his future, the two men finished discussing the details.

Within two weeks, Jack Dunn had worked out

a contract and signed George, who was to leave St. Mary's right away. He was excited about playing professional ball, but also sad about leaving the school, the only real home he had ever known. George said good-bye to all his friends and to the Brothers. His final good-bye was to Brother Matthias who, after all these years, had grown closer to him than his real father. They shook hands firmly. Then Brother Matthias pulled George in a little closer, winked and said, "You'll make it, George."

George grabbed his tiny suitcase. He stepped outside the iron gates and into the street where a wonderful new world awaited him. He was almost a man, he was free, and best of all, he was a Baltimore Oriole. He took his first train ride and joined the team in North Carolina for spring training.

George Ruth's impact on professional baseball was almost immediate. In his first game, Ruth,

Best of All, a Baltimore Oriole

playing shortstop, belted a tremendous home run that the fans buzzed was the longest shot they'd ever seen. Newspaper accounts said that the ball was hit so far that George "walked around the bases" while the ball was retrieved from a cornfield outside the ballpark.

A week later the young lefty took the hill in an exhibition game against the mighty Philadelphia Athletics of the American League, winners of three recent World Series. Ruth beat them easily, pitching a complete game. His career looked to be off and running.

George was having fun off the field, too. He was told to order whatever he wanted from the hotel dining room. All he had to do was sign his name to the check. George loved to sit down to eat enormous quantities of food—steaks, chicken, and potatoes with plenty of gravy.

The other players were amused by the sight of

their rookie with the bottomless stomach and three or four full plates in front of him.

Compared to some of his college-educated and well-traveled teammates, George sometimes seemed like an overgrown kid. With his first paycheck he bought a bicycle and rode around with the local kids. Most of the older players on the Orioles had cars, and the sight of George riding his new bike had them in hysterics.

Jack Dunn was extra careful to protect George from pranks and teasing, and even from himself. Some of the veterans growled that George was nothing more than Dunn's baby, that "babe" seemed a better name for this big rookie southpaw than George. And so, after only a few weeks in professional baseball, George Herman Ruth became "Babe" forevermore.

The regular season opened with Babe on a tear, both at the bat and on the mound. Each time out the

Babe Ruth Was Destined to Be a Star.

wisecracking rookie became just a little more confident. By early June it was obvious to everyone that Babe Ruth was destined to be a major-league star. Jack Dunn upped his salary to $1800, as much as most of the veterans received.

A new league had recently started, the outlaw Federal League, and they were raiding the minors, trying to lure good players away. One team had even started playing in Baltimore. Jack Dunn was afraid that his young star could be enticed away by a higher salary, so Dunn paid him the most he could.

The Orioles were playing good ball, but despite having a homegrown star like Babe Ruth to root for, the crowds in Baltimore were unusually low that year. The Federal League's Terrapins were drawing some of the fans away, and times were tough for many people.

It wasn't long before the Orioles were in bad financial trouble. Though he had just assembled the best minor-league club of his career, Jack Dunn found that the only way to save the franchise was to sell some of his top players to the major leagues.

The Boston Red Sox were developing a contending team and their owner jumped at the chance to acquire top-flight pitching. The Red Sox purchased the contracts of the two best arms that the Orioles had—Babe and Ernie Shore. In fact, to save himself from ruin, Dunn was forced to sell seven of his eight starters.

With great regret, Dunn announced the news to his players and said his good-byes, handing Ruth a train ticket to Boston and wishing him good luck. But Dunn's misfortune was the next big turning point in Babe's young life.

In only a few short months, the kid from St. Mary's, once in awe of nearly everything, had won 14 games and was on his way to the major leagues to take on the best baseball players in the world.

A Train Ticket to Boston

Chapter 4

On to Boston

The Babe and Ernie Shore took the train up to Boston and made their way to Fenway Park to meet Sox player-manager Bill Carrigan. Carrigan didn't waste a minute trying out the Babe. He scheduled him to pitch that very same day against the last-place Cleveland Indians.

In the Babe's first-ever major-league at bat he struck out. Pitching in the seventh inning with a two-run lead, Ruth got into trouble and the score became tied. Carrigan lifted the Babe for a pinch hitter in the bottom half of the inning. Although the Sox later rallied for a 4–3 win, Babe had a no decision in his first major league start.

In his next start, Ruth faced the powerful Detroit Tigers. In the fourth inning, with the game close and men on base, Carrigan saw something he didn't like about the way Babe was throwing and lifted him without explanation. The Tigers kept the lead and Ruth was charged with his first defeat.

After that he sat on the bench. His Oriole pal Ernie Shore was pitching well and had been moved into the starting rotation. Babe rode the pines for nearly four weeks before getting into another game. The always confident Ruth began to wonder if he was destined for failure.

Since his catching days at St. Mary's, the Babe had loved to hit. But pitchers were not supposed to take up time at batting practice; this was reserved for the regulars. Still, one day Ruth rushed up to the

Sawed Off at the Handle

cage to get in a little batting practice. He wanted to keep his batting eye sharp, hoping that Carrigan would at least use him as a pinch hitter.

One of the veterans growled, "Hey, rook, where do you think you're going? This is reserved for real players who play every day. We don't let pitchers waste our time, so beat it, kid!"

Ruth was infuriated. He almost lost his temper as he muscled his way past a few players and took some cuts anyway.

A few days later when the Babe went to the bat rack, he found that his bat had been sawed off at the handle. All the players in the dugout offered mock sympathy. In those days players were responsible for paying for their own equipment. It didn't seem like anything was going right.

The last blow was when Carrigan called Ruth into his office and announced that he was sending him down to the minors for a "little seasoning."

BABE RUTH

Ruth was to report to the Providence Grays. They played in the same International League as Jack Dunn's Baltimore Orioles.

Ruth joined a team which was locked in a tight pennant race. His pitching debut was against second-place Rochester. The matchup drew the largest crowd ever to attend a baseball game in Rhode Island. The fans were screaming at every pitch, and the Babe didn't disappoint them. Besides pitching a solid game, with the Grays trailing 4–2 in the ninth, Ruth hit a tremendous triple to drive in run number three. He scored on another triple and the Grays won the game, staying in first place.

The Babe went on to win nine games in just over a month during Providence's pennant-winning stretch drive, and he batted nearly .300. But the best part of Babe Ruth's rookie season was yet to come.

He Scored on a Triple.

Chapter 5

Hitting and Pitching

The morning after the Grays' final game, the Babe was awakened early by a knock at his hotel room door. He stumbled to the door in his nightshirt and opened it. To his surprise there stood a young, wide-eyed messenger holding out a tattered slip of paper.

"George Ruth?" inquired the boy.

As Babe sleepily nodded, the paper was pushed into his hand. By the time he looked up to thank him, the boy had vanished down the quiet hallway.

BABE RUTH

It was a telegram from Carrigan, ordering Babe to report back to the Red Sox immediately. Ruth got dressed and stuffed his tattered suitcase. He hailed a cab and rode to the railroad station where he caught the express train to Boston. He didn't even stop off for his customary extra-large breakfast.

There was more than one reason that Babe was so eager to rush back to Boston. Of course, he was thrilled to be back in the major leagues, and he was determined that this time he would stay there for good. But he was also happy because he wanted to see his girlfriend, Helen, who worked as a coffee-shop waitress in the hotel where the Red Sox players lived.

Ruth hadn't known Helen for very long, but had already become very fond of her. He had even taken a few expensive cab rides from Providence back to Boston on his off days just to see her for a few hours. Life was lonely for a young ballplayer on the road

The Best Friend He Ever Had

and so far from home, and Helen was the best friend that Babe had ever had.

With a week left in the regular season, Carrigan decided to let Ruth pitch against the New York Yankees, and Babe turned in a fine performance, winning the game and getting his first major league hit.

His long rookie season was finally over. Babe Ruth, pitching for three teams in 1914, had won a grand total of 28 games while losing only nine, quite a year in any league! It was even more remarkable considering that he had missed almost an entire month of play, when Carrigan had kept him on the bench!

Babe sat slumped in the clubhouse after the final Red Sox game. The locker room was noisy with players shouting out good-byes as they busily packed their gear. They couldn't wait to rejoin their families. Most of them had winter jobs to get to—for in those days baseball players were not well paid.

The Babe had decided to spend the off-season back in Baltimore helping his dad run the saloon. But he felt bad about leaving Helen behind.

That evening at the restaurant, after wolfing down a pile of pork chops and potatoes, a glum Babe suddenly came up with a grand solution. Why not get married, he decided!

When he proposed, Helen eagerly said yes, and they left for Baltimore immediately. A week later they were married.

The winter passed quickly, and soon he was saying good-bye to his father and Helen and joining the Red Sox at their training camp in Arkansas. He wouldn't see his wife again until the regular season started in Boston.

Manager Carrigan liked the looks of his 1915 Red Sox squad, especially in the pitching department. But despite Babe's talent, in the exhibition

They Were Married.

games, he was wild and unsteady. It was another rookie, Carl Mays, who caught Carrigan's eye that spring. Because the Sox had plenty of established lefties, by opening day Babe was slated as the fifth, irregular starter. But the Red Sox started the season poorly. The starters came up with injuries and the talented mound staff was, for the moment, crippled. Carrigan found that he indeed needed his big lefty.

It was Babe's big chance to reestablish himself, and he didn't waste a moment. His first few performances were good enough to put him back in Carrigan's good graces. But it was his bat that began to raise a few eyebrows around the league.

At this time in baseball history, to win, a team had to master the "inside game," a combination of good pitching, solid defense, and hitting fundamentals. The home run was not the potent weapon that it is today. A stolen base, a sacrifice and a smoothly stroked base hit behind the runner were considered far more important to winning than an occasional home run.

These years would later become known as the "dead ball" era. The baseballs themselves were not made as well as they are today and the pitchers were in command. Only one ball was used for each game. After five or six innings the balls were often ripped and battered. Pitchers were allowed to scuff the balls and darken them with tobacco juice or grease, making them hop strangely and hard to see.

Homers were few and far between. The newspapers barely bothered to report on home runs, and some writers worried that too many of them would ruin baseball, even though, in 1914, "too many" wasn't really much at all. The American League leaders, Sam Crawford and Frank "Home Run" Baker, had hit only eight apiece! But that was about to change.

High to Right Field

BABE RUTH

Early on, Babe faced the New York Yankees. Batting in the third inning, Ruth lashed a tremendous home run. It was Babe's first major home run ever, but no one thought much about it. Later that month, the Red Sox again visited New York. Before the game, the players were checking the lineup cards in the dugout. One of them called out, "Hey, Babe, watch out, it's Warhop on the mound." It was Warhop who had given up that monster homer to Ruth.

Ruth looked out on the field and saw Jack Warhop warming up for the Yanks. Carrigan sidled up to Babe and told him to watch out. He knew that a crusty old veteran like Warhop hated to be shown up and might intentionally throw at the young star to get even. In those days players were tough, hard men. They played the game with a kind of fury that is not seen in today's player.

Sure enough, when Babe stepped in, Warhop's

first pitch sailed inside and under his chin. But Babe didn't back down. On the next pitch he took a mighty rip and slammed it high to right field. The outfielder took only a few steps back and then stopped, watching as the ball sailed clear over the roof of the Polo Grounds.

Babe had hit this one even further than the first! He capped off the day by pitching a strong five-hitter as the Red Sox cruised to a 5–1 victory.

In late June, Ruth hit a ball at Fenway Park to a spot high in the bleachers that had been reached only once before. Later that summer he launched a rocket completely out of the stadium in St. Louis. His strong pitching and hitting helped propel the Red Sox into first place and to the pennant. He finished the year 18–8 and batted .315.

But it was his four home runs that were the talk of the town. Although homers were considered just another hit, no better than a single, Babe's

Pitching a Strong Five-Hitter

home runs stirred interest because of their spectac-ular distance. In his first full season, Babe had hit four of the longest homers anyone had ever seen! And, as he loved to point out to anyone who would listen, he had hit them in only 92 at bats, far short of the four to five hundred at bats that the everyday players got.

The powerful Red Sox pitching staff, led by Ruth, Mays, and two 19-game winners, Shore and Rube Foster, was ready for the 1915 World Series to begin. The Red Sox played the Philadelphia Phillies, led by pitching legend Grover Cleveland Alexander. "Alexander the Great," as he was known, had won 31 games that year. The Phils also had Gavvy Cra-vath, who had led the National League in RBIs and who had set a new record for home runs that year with 24.

Babe figured that he'd play an important role in the Series, but Carrigan had other ideas. Babe had pitched a complete game only two days before the Series opened. Carrigan had decided to use him only in an emergency. Although Babe begged to pitch in the Series, Carrigan wouldn't change his mind. Pinch hitting in the ninth inning of the first game, Ruth grounded out and the Red Sox lost 3–1.

That was the only appearance Babe Ruth made in his first Series. His teammates won the next four games.

The Red Sox were the world champs and Babe, although greatly disappointed that he didn't pitch, heartily joined in the celebration. Babe's Series bonus money was even more than his year's salary!

Spirits Were High.

Chapter 6

The Legend Begins

Beantown was bubbling with excitement over the prospects for the 1916 season. The Red Sox seemed like a good bet to repeat as American League champs. During spring training, the players' spirits were high. Some of the optimism ended when the team's owner, Joseph Lannin, decided to sell some of his high-salaried veterans to save some money.

Thinking that his great pitching staff and tight defense would carry the team, Lannin shocked everyone by selling batting star Tris Speaker to the Cleveland Indians. In addition to his .343 lifetime average, Speaker was renowned for his defense. Playing a shallow center field, he occasionally got involved in base path rundowns. More than once he made unassisted double plays by catching a fly ball to center and racing in to tag the runner caught off base!

Early on, the Red Sox were stuck in third place, but Babe was having a fine season. He hit three homers in three games and edged the American League's best pitcher, Walter Johnson of the Senators, 1–0.

But the fortunes of the team began to change. By late July, the Red Sox were in a tight pennant race with Ty Cobb's Detroit Tigers and the Chicago White Sox led by Eddie Collins and "Shoeless" Joe Jackson.

In August, with only a few games separating

Babe Was Having a Fine Season.

the three teams in the standings, Babe again bested Johnson 1–0, matching him pitch for pitch in a thirteen-inning thriller. Despite Carrigan's insistence on batting Babe ninth, in the traditional pitcher's spot in the order, Babe's average climbed above .300, for a while the highest on the team.

In September, with every game important, Ruth out-dueled Johnson for the fifth time that season! The newspapers were now heralding Babe as having the league's best arm.

When the Red Sox arrived in Chicago for a showdown, the hometown White Sox fans jammed into Comisky Park to form the largest crowd ever to see a game in the Windy City. Babe knew that the season was on the line. The high-flying White Sox boasted a formidable lineup. The spirited crowd roared for their team, but the crafty Ruth easily mowed through the Chicago lineup, winning his 20th game of the year 6–2. The next day, Ernie

Shore hurled the Red Sox to another win. Boston moved into first place.

The Red Sox edged out the White Sox by two games to clinch the pennant. Ruth finished the year winning his 23rd game by shutting out the Yankees. Babe's nine shutouts and his 1.75 earned run average (ERA) led the American League. His shutout performance was a league record for southpaws until Yankee hurler Ron Guidry tied that mark sixty-two years later.

The National League champions, the Brooklyn Robins (later to become the Dodgers) were the Red Sox's opponents in the World Series. Ernie Shore got the Red Sox started with an opening game win.

Before game two, Carrigan called Babe into his office. "Babe, I'm giving you the ball tomorrow. Go out there and do your best for me, kid," he told Ruth.

Babe saw a glint of sadness in his manager's worn expression. "What's the matter skipper, feelin'

"I've Been Catching Since You Were Born."

under the weather today?" he asked.

"No, Babe, I'm just fine. But you know, I've been in baseball a mighty long time. I've been catching since the time you were born, and then these last few years I've had to run around keeping you young fellas in line. I'm getting tired, Babe, just plain worn out . . . and I've decided this is it. After the Series I'm gonna retire."

Ruth was stunned. The last few years he had grown both to admire and respect his hard-bitten manager. He was to say later in life that Carrigan was the best leader he had ever known.

Ruth started to speak, but Carrigan interrupted. "Save it, Babe, my mind's made up. But I want to tell you something." Carrigan paused as his memories floated by. "I've seen 'em all come and go, Cy Young, Christy Mathewson, Kid Nichols . . . all the greats. Don't forget that I was the catcher when the Sox won it all in 1912. I was there when Smoky

Joe Wood won his 34 games that year . . . sixteen of 'em in a row! And there was no man alive that could bring it faster than Smoky Joe.

"But you could be the best yet, Babe, the best of 'em all. Send me out a winner, Babe." Carrigan gave Babe a good luck pat and sent him outside to join the others.

Babe sat on the bench turning a fresh new baseball round in his hand. He was even more determined than ever to make this game something special. It was a misty, damp day; dark rain clouds hung in the outfield sky. But this game turned out to be one of the brightest moments in young Babe's career.

After Babe got the first two batters out, the third man up hit a long drive to center. The Boston outfielder tripped as he turned for the catch. The ball rolled all the way to the outfield wall. The throw back to the infield was also bobbled and the runner

"You Could Be the Best, Babe."

slid into home ahead of the throw for an inside-the-park home run. The Babe knocked in a run in the bottom of the third to tie the game. As the game went along, Ruth seemed stronger and more confident every inning. The Red Sox just missed winning in the bottom of the ninth but had a man thrown out at the plate for the third out!

The Boston fans were on the edge of their seats as the game went into extra innings. By the fourteenth inning, it was getting very dark and the hitters were having a hard time seeing the ball. In the home half of the fourteenth, a pinch-hit single broke the deadlock. The Red Sox had win number two. Babe had pitched fourteen remarkable innings, giving up no hits to the Dodgers after the seventh inning. It was one of the most exciting World Series games ever.

In the jubilant Red Sox clubhouse, Babe was hopping up and down like a little kid on Christmas morning. He hugged his teammates. Then he grabbed Carrigan and held him up in the air with his massive arms.

"I told you a year ago I could take care of those National League bums, and you never gave me a chance!" exclaimed Babe.

Carrigan, with a twinkle in his eye, grabbed Babe's arm and said, "Forget it, Babe. You made monkeys out of them today. It was a game none of us will ever forget."

The Red Sox proved to be unstoppable now, wrapping up the Series in five games. Babe never got a second chance to pitch as Ernie Shore pitched a three-hitter in the finale, and the Red Sox had won their second consecutive championship!

The Red Sox Started Fast.

Chapter 7

Baseball's Bad Boy

By the time the Red Sox came to spring training in 1917, some serious changes had taken place. The club owner had sold the team to Broadway show producer Harry Frazee, and Frazee then hired former Athletics shortstop Jack Barry to manage. Barry inherited a pitching staff that had accounted for 192 regular season wins over the past two years. The team seemed all set to win their third straight championship.

The Red Sox started fast. By late May, Ruth had

already won ten games! Then came one of the oddest episodes in Babe's career. It began as an ordinary start against the Washington Senators at Fenway Park. The first batter of the game took his stance and Babe fired a pitch that looked pretty good to him as it nipped the outside corner of the plate.

The umpire raised his right arm to signal ball one. Babe shook his head and looked to the heavens in mock protest over the call. He went into his windup and again delivered. The ump cried "Ball two!"

As the catcher returned the ball, Ruth took a few steps toward the plate and peered at the umpire.

"What are you, blind?" Babe muttered, now obviously upset.

"Hey you big lug, get back on that mound, keep your mouth shut, and pitch!" the umpire snarled back.

Babe went back, kicked the rubber and some

"Ball Two!"

dirt, and then stood with his back to the plate look-ing out at Harry Hooper in right field. There he stood fuming, while pounding the baseball into his glove time after time.

"Play ball, Ruth," the umpire bellowed, and Babe reared back and fired the hardest fast ball that he could.

"Ball three!" came the call back just as fast. The Babe was really steaming now. He had never seen such lousy umpiring, even at St. Mary's!

Again Babe paced around the mound, kicking up dust and waving his arms. The infielders shifted nervously and stretched, waiting for the game to resume. Babe then fired his fourth pitch; there was no doubt it was ball four. Nonetheless, the call enraged him.

Babe walked toward home plate, eyes glaring. The umpire yelled for him to get back and pitch or he would be thrown out of the game. From the Senators dugout came catcalls and whistles. Someone yelled, "Hey, Ruth, you're a bum!"

"You toss me and I'll bust you in the nose!" shouted Babe, shaking his fist at the umpire.

The umpire, mask in hand, gestured toward the dugout and yelled, "You're outta here, Ruth... finished!"

Babe tried to get at the umpire as manager Barry and the catcher did their best to hold him off, but then Babe broke free and socked the umpire right on the jaw! A policeman suddenly arrived on the field and the three managed to escort Babe away before he got into even more trouble.

Ernie Shore was summoned in to take over. On the first pitch, the base runner took off trying to steal second, but a strong throw nailed him easily. Unbelievably, Shore then proceeded to retire the next twenty-six Senators in a row for a perfect no-hit, no-run game—only the fourth

"Tape-Measure Home Runs"

time it had ever been done!

The next day, Babe was as sorry as could be. He didn't know what had gotten into him. However, the president of the league took an even dimmer view of his bad behavior. Babe was suspended for a few days and fined.

Nonetheless, the Babe had another terrific year, pitching 25 complete games and winning 24 of them. Only Ty Cobb, George Sisler and ex-team-mate Tris Speaker had bettered his .325 batting average. As was becoming his trademark, Ruth had belted a few "tape-measure" home runs the likes of which had never been seen before.

Chapter 8

Wins and Losses

By the spring of 1918, the United States had entered the first World War. Troops were needed for an army that was fighting in France. Boston manager Jack Barry joined the Navy, and Ed Barrow was hired as the new manager.

The Red Sox still had a formidable pitching staff led by Babe and Carl Mays, who had won 22 games the year before. But the hitting was still a weak spot. Babe was clearly the team's best hitter, though he continued to bat in the ninth slot. As the

A Formidable Pitching Staff

season moved into early summer, no one else on the team was even batting .300, yet Babe only appeared every fourth or fifth game when it was his turn to pitch, or occasionally as a pinch hitter.

One reporter pointed out that attendance at the games always swelled when Babe was scheduled to play. The fans were coming to the ballpark more to see him hit than pitch. The hope of seeing one of Babe's monster clouts was a major attraction both at Fenway Park and on the road.

Even some of the Red Sox players privately suggested to Barrow that he try Babe at a regular position. One of them was Harry Hooper, a terrific outfielder and captain of the team. Hooper was the heart and soul of the Red Sox, and the leadoff hitter for three other champion Red Sox teams. His sensational bare-handed catch of a sure home run saved the final game in the 1912 Series, and his two homers won the final game of the 1915 World series.

He was a well-spoken college graduate and a student of the game, and Barrow often conferred with him on strategy during games.

"Listen, skipper, we've got plenty of good pitching, probably the best in the league. But the boys don't think we'll ever take the flag without more hitting. Why can't you try using Babe as an outfielder?" Hooper pleaded. "He's the best bat we've got!"

At first, the stubborn Barrow, a strict believer in the "inside game" that stressed good pitching, wouldn't consider the move. The manager thought that a well-pitched game was far more important than a few home runs. "I'll be the laughingstock of the American League if I take my best pitcher and put him in the outfield. It's out of the question!" Barrow stormed.

Barrow tried shuffling various players in and out of the lineup. but none of them could deliver a

The Big Crowds

big hit like Babe. The team, especially with Speaker gone, was slumping for lack of hitting.

One afternoon after a close loss, Barrow sat in his office. He knew that he would have to do something to turn the team around. He began thinking about what Hooper had said. That very day, Ruth had supplied nearly all of Boston's offense with a long homer. As a part-owner of the team, Barrow realized that the big crowds coming every time Babe played would mean more profit from ticket sales. Why not give it a try, he decided.

Barrow found Babe at the hotel restaurant sitting before a mountain of hot dogs piled on a plate. Babe was so busy eating, he didn't see Barrow standing in front of him. The manager cleared his throat loudly and then Babe looked up.

"What's up, skipper?" asked Babe, his usual way of addressing the manager, or "skipper" of his team.

Barrow pushed back his straw hat, straightened his tie and sat down.

"Listen, Babe," he said. "I've been thinking. You're big and strong. And you're the best hitter I've got. I've decided to let you play another position on the days when you're not pitching. I think it would be a grand move to help the team, and the fans would love it too."

"Why, that'd be sensational, skip," Babe answered after another bite of hot dog, his round face breaking into that big boyish grin. "When do I start?"

"Right away, Babe," Barrow said, "but you have to promise me one thing. You have to be ready to pitch for me, and take your regular turn as long as I need you, okay?"

Babe nodded in agreement. The very next day, Babe Ruth was in the Red Sox lineup at first base. Barrow looked like a genius as Babe

"When Do I Start?"

hit a homer and played his position flawlessly. The next day batting cleanup, he hit another. The experiment was looking pretty good as Babe continued to batter American League pitching, hitting nearly .500!

Since the Red Sox already had a solid first baseman, Stuffy McInnis, Barrow soon shifted Babe to left field where he played except for the days he pitched.

He was pitching pretty well too, on pace to win his usual 20 games, when he fell dangerously ill.

Babe had developed a bad cold, and then a sore throat. His fever got so high that he couldn't pitch his regular start. He nearly collapsed in the clubhouse and ended up in the hospital for a week with a worried Helen sitting beside his bed. There were even rumors that he would die. But in two weeks he was well enough to return to the lineup.

He returned with a bang, belting four round-trippers in his first four games back! How he loved to hit!

Unfortunately Babe found that he had lost his love of pitching. But he kept his promise to Barrow and stayed in the rotation. Then, after three tough losses in a row, he was sulking. Barrow was concerned with his lefty's slump. After all, the Red Sox were neck and neck with the Indians for the lead, and he knew he would need Babe Ruth on the mound as the season drew to a close.

Babe was already telling a few teammates and reporters that he was planning on skipping a few starts to concentrate on his outfield play. One day after hearing him complain about what a chore it was to pitch, Barrow blew up and called Babe into his office.

Barrow wasn't like the typical manager. He made no effort to be a friend of the players like Carrigan had. Barrow didn't care if he was liked or not,

"My Pitching Days Are Behind Me!"

as long as the team won. Baseball was all business to him. He didn't even dress in a uniform, preferring to wear a suit and tie while managing. Above all, he was tough—he had been in baseball a long time—and wasn't about to let any player call the shots on his team, not even the star.

"Listen, Ruth," cautioned the stern Barrow, his eyes narrowing, "we had a deal. You play and hit, but you pitch when I want—you get the picture? I don't like what I'm hearing from the reporters."

Babe did not wear his customary grin. "It won't work," Babe insisted. "Pitching ain't fun any more. I like the feel of the bat in my hands, not the ball! I don't care about the agreement. I'm an outfielder now. My pitching days are behind me. I ain't takin' the mound any more!"

Barrow reminded Babe that he was under contract and that he'd better pitch when he had to. Babe threatened to quit the team if he didn't get his way. He stormed out of the office in a rage, leaving Barrow fuming.

As stubborn as he was, the manager knew he needed Babe to win. He hoped that it was just a matter of time before Babe changed his mind. First he tried to use some of his other pitchers in Babe's spot.

Dutch Leonard pitched well enough to become the ace of the staff for a while. In June, Leonard hurled a no-hitter and reeled off three straight shutouts. But then, without explanation, Leonard bolted from the team to go work in the Boston shipyards and pitch for their semipro team. With his pay as a shipyard worker plus extra pay for being on the semipro team, a player could often make as much money as he could playing in the majors. Barrow was stuck again and the Red Sox were soon bumped out of first place.

Barrow called Babe back into his office. He

He Stormed Out in a Rage.

asked, almost pleaded with him to pitch. Babe insisted that he would not. Besides, he added, his wrist was hurting, a claim that the skeptical Barrow refused to believe. Again tempers flared, and the agitated Barrow ordered Babe to start against the Yankees.

The next day Ruth appeared in the dugout with his wrist wrapped up and a pained expression on his face. The infuriated Barrow ripped down the lineup card and crossed out Babe Ruth's name. But the regular Sox center fielder came up lame that day, and Barrow was forced to use Babe in the field. Ruth promptly hit his ninth home run of the year.

By midseason Babe had stroked 11 dingers. The newspapers began to refer to him as the "Home Run King". Reports on games gave special attention to whether Babe had hit one out, something done for no other player. The press and the public had caught the first case of home run fever—everyone except

Barrow, that is. He continued to insist that Babe take the hill. Feelings got so bad that the two men barely spoke to one another.

One day, after a loss, their tempers exploded as never before. Babe had missed a take sign, and when he got to the dugout, Barrow met him on the first step.

"Hey, Ruth, that was a bum play," said Barrow as he shook his head in disgust. The players all stopped in their tracks to watch.

Babe's eyes opened wide. He had been embarrassed in front of his teammates. "Don't you call me a bum unless you'd like a nice punch in the nose!" he said.

Barrow, gazing steadily past Babe, and onto the field added, "That'll cost you $500 smackers, wise guy, and—"

But before he could utter another word, Ruth flung his bat on the ground in disgust. "The heck it

"I Quit!"

will!" screamed a red-faced Babe, loud enough for the fans in the first section to hear clearly. "I quit!"

With that, he stormed off the field. The game continued and one inning later, Barrow sent the batboy into the clubhouse to find Babe.

"He's gone. He dressed and left," said the clubhouse attendant.

The players were stunned. After the game, Babe was nowhere to be found. He had checked out of the hotel and was already on his way to Big George's tavern in Baltimore. The next morning, a reporter sent Barrow a telegram saying that Babe was getting ready to sign a contract with a shipyard team in Pennsylvania. By the afternoon, the news was a headline in every paper.

Some smart reporters tracked Babe down and found him resting at his father's place. By then he had calmed down considerably. He admitted that once again his temper had gotten the best of him.

"I didn't want to fight, I just want to play baseball and have fun. Things are getting so complicated!" Babe told the reporters. He added that he would be ready to rejoin the team in a few days . . . if Barrow wanted him back.

Babe made his way back to Boston. At another meeting, he and Barrow reached a compromise: Babe would be allowed to play the outfield, but every fourth day he would pitch.

This was just the spark the Red Sox needed. Playing every day and batting cleanup, Babe went on a hitting tear. The team surged into first place. On one road trip, showing some real hustle, he hit five triples in only seven games!

One Sunday afternoon late in the season, a day when the Red Sox had no game to play, Babe and Helen decided to go on a picnic. Just before they were about to leave, they received a telegram.

"Probably more congratulations on my great

"I Want to Play Baseball and Have Fun!"

year," Babe laughed to Helen as he opened it. But suddenly Babe's eyes welled up with tears. He sat down trembling. Helen looked at the message. Babe's father, Big George, had fallen, hit his head, and died.

Babe and Helen immediately caught a train to Baltimore and attended the funeral. At the ceremony, while the preacher spoke, Babe closed his eyes and thought back on his childhood. Although times had been rough, and his relationship with Big George had had its ups and downs, Babe had truly loved his dad and would miss him.

Later Babe went over to the darkened tavern and looked around. He could almost feel the ghosts of the past still lingering. He remembered the clank of the honky-tonk piano, and the smells of tobacco and beer. They were now gone forever. This was no longer his home.

Helen touched his shoulder, and he awoke as if

from a dream. He remembered that he had a job to finish back in Boston; perhaps another World Series to play. He turned, locked the door and walked away. The next morning he was back in uniform at Fenway.

A few days later he was on the mound pitching the Sox to victory over the Athletics. This win clinched the pennant for Boston. Although the Babe's record had dropped to 13–7, seven of those wins had come during the final month of the season. He ended up hitting an even .300, and had shared the league lead in homers with 11. More than half of his hits had been for extra bases!

The Red Sox were set to square off with the weak–hitting National League champions, the Chicago Cubs. Everyone in Boston wondered if Barrow would open the Series with Babe Ruth on the mound. Barrow himself seemed to change his mind every other day. Once he told some reporters that

A Mighty Roar Went Up.

Ruth probably wouldn't pitch at all!

On the day of the game, Barrow had two other pitchers warming up. It looked like 21-game winner Mays would get the nod. But when the Red Sox trotted out to their positions, a mighty roar went up as Babe Ruth slowly walked to the mound, holding the baseball.

Babe pitched a crafty five-hitter and shut down the Cubs, 1–0. That night on the train ride back to Boston, Babe and some of the players were horsing around. Babe accidentally banged his left hand and the next morning his fingers were swollen to twice their size. Babe kept the injury to himself.

Still hurting, Babe pitched again in the fourth game, taking a 2–0 lead into the sixth. The Red Sox had scored two runs on a clutch Ruth triple that bounced off the center field wall. The Boston fans were jumping for joy. After Babe mowed down three more Cubs in the seventh, there was a distinct buzzing in the hometown crowd.

"What the heck's going on up there?" Barrow asked the team.

"Don't you know?" answered one of the players. "Babe's just broken Christy Mathewson's record for scoreless innings in a row!"

When the Cubs finally punched home a run in the eighth, the string was broken. Dating back to the 1916 Series against Brooklyn, Babe Ruth had pitched 29 2/3 innings of scoreless baseball. It was a moment that the Babe would cherish forever. The record lasted until 1962 when Whitey Ford racked up 33 2/3 innings for the Yankees.

In typical Red Sox fashion, the game was won in the eighth frame as Boston scored a run on a passed ball and wild throw. Babe, with a little help from reliever Joe Bush, had his second win of the Series.

Boston defeated the Cubs four games to two as

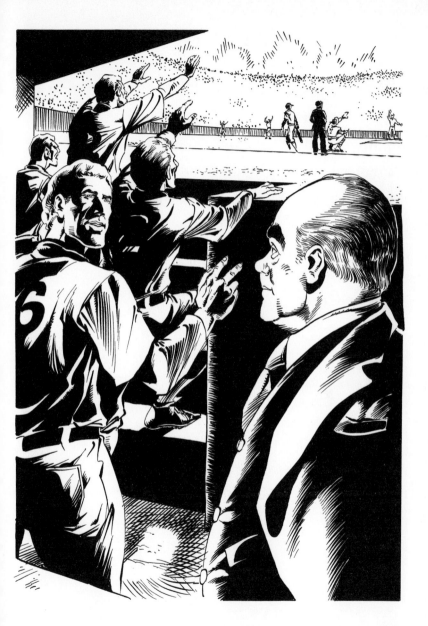

"Babe's Just Broken Mathewson's Record!"

Carl Mays tripped up the Cubbies 2–1, pitching a sterling three-hitter in the finale. The Red Sox were champions again! With that great pitching staff and the Babe knocking the ball out of the park, the sportswriters proclaimed a Boston dynasty! The Red Sox could probably win a row of championships in the years to come. After all, what team could stop them?

Chapter 9

Setting and Breaking Records

Babe Ruth had become famous on and off the field. Most Bostonians learned of his exploits in the newspapers. Even when he didn't clout a home run or pitch a great game, stories would appear about what Babe ate, where he went and even how he spent his money.

He could entertain a crowd just by showing up and saying a few words. He never worried about giving his opinion on anything, even on subjects that he didn't know anything about! He could sometimes

"Hot, Ain't It, Prez?"

be very loud and was always very funny, a real showman with a twinkle in his eye and time for everyone.

One funny thing about Babe was that he couldn't remember people's names—even those of players around the league and on his own team, men he'd known for years! Instead, he called everyone "kid," which, with his Baltimore waterfront accent, sounded more like "keed." "Hiya, keed" was his usual greeting to men, women, children and even shocked senators and judges!

Most people would get tongue-tied when introduced to the president of the United States, but when Babe met Warren Harding before a ball game, he leaned in and remarked, "Hot as hell today, ain't it, Prez?"

His fellow players loved him as much as the public did. They could depend on him to play every inning of every game hard, and to win. He kept the team loose and relaxed. He took the blame when things went wrong and readily shared the glory of winning.

Though Babe enjoyed being famous, he soon found it impossible to go anywhere without drawing a crowd. Figuring that Boston would be their home for as long as he played baseball, Babe and Helen bought a farm in the country where they could go to relax.

Before the next season began, Barrow reminded Babe of the compromise they had made the year before, that Babe was expected to pitch regularly. Neither man trusted the other, and it was an uneasy truce.

The Red Sox opened the season on the road. Barrow had decided to room Babe with one of his trusted coaches, who could keep on eye on him. Despite the fact that Babe was hitting a ton and was his best player, the straight-arrow Barrow couldn't

A Farm in the Country

stand Babe's late hours and fun-loving ways. He was determined to put an end to them, no matter what.

One night Barrow gave the hotel porter a few dollars and told him to wake him when Babe came in, no matter how late it was. When Babe slipped in at 6 A.M. and went to his room, Barrow was awakened by the porter. He put on his robe and crept up to Ruth's door. He saw a crack of light coming from under the door. Then he stiffened as he heard voices, and then laughing.

Barrow knocked and the light went out; all was quiet. Barrow opened the unlocked door and walked in. When he turned on the light he was startled to see Babe lying innocently in bed, eyes closed and the blanket pulled up tight to his chin.

Barrow's eyes narrowed as he saw one hand sticking out of the covers holding a smoking pipe! The other bed was empty, the trusted coach having fled into the bathroom to hide. Babe slowly opened one eye.

"Well, Babe," said Barrow, a knowing smile on his face. "I'm glad to see that you're getting your rest." He began to turn away, but looked back. "By the way, Babe, do you always smoke a pipe this early in the morning?" he asked.

"You bet," answered Babe. "It's a great way to relax." Babe gave his most sincere smile.

Barrow walked over to the bed and yanked off the covers.

There lay a completely dressed Babe. Even his shoes were still on! Barrow, his bushy eyebrows twitching up and down, stormed out of the room and slammed the door.

Later at the ballpark, Barrow called a team meeting to discuss rules. Every so often he would shoot a glance at Babe while talking to the others about "bad apples in the barrel" and the importance

"He's Not Human!"

of getting enough sleep and staying in good condition.

In a flash Babe was calling Barrow all sorts of names and threatening to punch him in the nose. Barrow had no choice but to suspend him again.

"I don't know what I'm going to do with that young hothead," Barrow confided to one of the coaches. "Trouble is that he's not like any ordinary player I've ever managed. Did you ever see anyone else who could stay out all night and still hit two home runs? He's not human!"

After that afternoon's game, which Babe sat out, he went to Barrow's office. "I'm really sorry for what happened today, Mr. Barrow," said an embarrassed Babe.

"It's time that you straightened yourself out, Babe," cautioned the manager. "I know you had it tough as a kid but you can't go around calling people names and threatening to punch them. You're a grown man and there's a lot of people counting on you. Kids look up to you. It's time to start leading a decent life."

Babe hung his head and nodded in agreement. He would follow all the rules if Barrow would lift the suspension and let him play—playing baseball was far more important to him than going to parties could ever be. A relieved Barrow agreed to take back his star.

But despite the new understanding between Ruth and his manager, the Red Sox were having a terrible year. Even Barrow realized that the strain of pitching and playing every day was wearing Babe out, extra sleep or not. Babe was now considered an outfielder first, a pitcher second. But nothing Barrow did could bring back the glory of the past years. The Red Sox continued to slide, ending up in sixth place.

Ruth, however, produced one of the greatest

"Kids Look Up to You."

seasons of personal bests ever. He won nine games pitching that year, but he won many more with his bat. By early July he had hit 11 homers, equaling his mark the year before. By late July, he had smashed his 16th. The blast tied the American League record set by "Socks" Seybold back in 1902 when Babe was only seven years old.

His assault on the record book didn't stop there. In September, Babe hit number 25, passing the modern Major League mark set by his former World Series opponent, Gavvy Cravath of the 1915 Phillies. He finished the season with 29 homeruns and batted .322.

Babe hit at least one homer in each ballpark he played in, something that had never been done before. His four grand slammers set a mark that would stand until the 1960s. Sportswriters proclaimed him the greatest home run hitter ever, standing head and shoulders above the rest. He was truly the first superstar of sports.

Although Red Sox owner Harry Frazee had baseball's version of Superman in Babe Ruth and the game's biggest attraction, he was almost broke. He liked to spend his money producing Broadway shows, many of which were flops. Now, just as Jack Dunn of the Baltimore Orioles had done years ago, Frazee found the best way to get some quick cash was by selling off his best players.

During the off-season, the players heard grumbling that Frazee would dump some of the older and well-paid among them. But no one dreamed that Frazee would make what would prove to be the worst deal in the history of baseball. Frazee managed to blame Babe for Boston's poor 1919 finish, unjustly calling him selfish and out of control.

He then stunned Babe, the Boston fans and nearly everyone connected with baseball by announcing in the spring of 1920 that he had sold

One Hundred Thousand Dollars!

BABE RUTH

Babe Ruth to the New York Yankees for an astounding $100,000! Frazee also unloaded Ernie Shore, Carl Mays and a few other Red Sox stars.

The sale marked the decline of the great Boston team. The Red Sox had won five of the first fifteen World Series, but now, seventy-seven years after their last win in 1918, the team has not won another World Series. Generations of Red Sox fans have come to refer to this terrible deal, and the drought of championships, as "The Curse of the Bambino." (Bambino, Italian for Babe, was another affectionate nickname given to Ruth.)

But as much as the sale hurt Boston, it benefited New York. The Yankee dynasty, one of the greatest in sports history, was about to begin.

Chapter 10

On to New York

Baseball had changed dramatically since Babe's rookie year. Gone forever was the close-knit "inside game." In 1920 the fans wanted home runs and lots of scoring. A new, livelier, cork-centered ball was introduced, marking the end of the "dead ball" era.

New rules had been made outlawing the spitball and making it illegal to tamper with the baseball in any way. Record numbers of fans were attending ball games and many came just to see

The Fans Wanted Home Runs.

BABE RUTH

America's new national hero, Babe Ruth.

But Babe was much more than a home run hitter. Today, most of what we see of Babe Ruth are grainy films and photos taken near the end of his career when he had eaten his way to a big belly and round face.

But in 1920, Babe, at 6' 2" tall and about 200 pounds, was slim-waisted and muscular. He had thick wrists and forearms with which he could send a ball flying, even when fooled into taking a bad pitch far out of the strike zone.

Many old-timers remember Babe's hitting homers on pitches both down at his shoelaces and up near the brim of his cap; he could hit out any pitch he could reach. In fact, his arms were so strong that he wielded a 52-ounce bat with a thin handle that came around like a whip. Most power-hitters today find it impossible to swing anything over 32 ounces!

BABE RUTH

On the field, he moved with speed and grace. Babe was a skillful and aggressive base runner who could leg out a triple, finishing it with a neat hook slide. He would steal 31 bases in his first two years with the Yanks, and stole 123 bases in his career, including home a few times.

Babe's fielding is often overlooked. His managers always pointed to his great baseball instincts, as he was always positioned correctly while patrolling right field. His arm was strong and accurate. He never threw to the wrong base and rarely missed the cutoff man. But the fans didn't turn out to see Babe run the bases or throw out runners. They came to see him hit.

Babe was a natural for New York, a city of excitement and celebrities. When the 1920 season opened, Babe didn't hit a homer until May. But his first came fittingly as the Yanks hosted the Red Sox. It was one of the longest Babe ever hit, traveling

His Trademark Home Run Trot

over the upper deck of the Polo Grounds.

After that, baseball was never the same. Ruth went into his trademark head-down-and-tiptoe-stepped home run trot 53 more times that year, belting more homers than any other *team* in the league had!

A 26-game batting streak sent his batting average to .376, putting the previously hapless Yankees into a tight pennant race with Cleveland.

Although the Yanks slipped and finished a close third, Babe had possibly the greatest single season ever for his new owner, Colonel Jacob Ruppert. Babe had scored 158 runs with 137 RBIs. All the great hitters that have come and gone since have never come close to matching his slugging average of .847 that year. Meanwhile the punchless Red Sox had fallen to fifth place with Harry Hooper leading the team in homers with a lowly seven!

There wasn't much that the American League

pitchers could do to stop Babe. They tried intentional walks and overshifts, but nothing worked. Some tried to throw only slow curve balls, hoping to frustrate him. He'd yell back at them to "get some mustard on it" and if they didn't, he'd reach out and slap a double to the opposite field.

Opposing managers had a standing rule that if Babe Ruth came to bat late in a game where he was in a position to beat you, you had to walk him, no exceptions. No batter in the history of the game was as feared as Babe.

Probably no other player faced as many bad pitches as the Babe did—his league-leading 148 walks in 142 games proves that. Just the sight of Babe striding to the plate could rattle even the best hurlers in the game.

Even when Babe didn't send a shot over the wall, his outs could be memorable. He gripped the

He'd Yell Back at Them.

bat tightly and swung with everything he had. Even his strikeouts were dramatic and brought gasps from the stands as he whipped his bat around like a tornado.

Once he popped a towering fly ball nearly straight up. The circling infielders became so dizzy that they lost the ball and it dropped between them. Babe, hustling all the way, ended up standing on third with a big smile.

When the Yankees began the 1921 season, Babe continued to destroy American League pitching. To Babe's dismay, Colonel Ruppert had signed on ex-Red Sox manager Ed Barrow as the Yankee's general manager. Although Barrow would no longer be checking Babe's bedtimes, he would prove to be as tough as ever when the Babe wanted more money.

But Barrow was a shrewd baseball man, great at trading for new talent while running a shipshape ball club. Yankee manager Miller Huggins and Barrow went right to work adding a few players here and there, and soon the Yankees were loaded. The pitching staff was led by Babe's former Red Sox teammate Carl Mays, who went on to win 27 games that year.

The heart of the Yankee lineup, with Ruth, Bob Meusel, Wally Pipp and Roger Peckinpaugh, gave American League pitchers constant trouble. It was the start of a fearsome Yankee attack that would last for decades.

Meusel was a star destined to play in Ruth's shadow. He was a great hitter, batting over .300 every year, and a terrific outfielder. No one in the league, not even great base runners like Ty Cobb, would ever challenge his rifle arm. He could catch a fly ball, and without even taking a step, throw all the way to the plate without a bounce! There are very few players who have done that even once, but

The Yankees Clinched the Flag.

for Meusel it was routine.

In mid-September Babe hit his 55th homer of the season, breaking his own record. The Yankees were in a dogfight with the Cleveland Indians, led by Babe's ex-Boston teammate and now archrival, Tris Speaker. Each team took turns in first place. The race came down to a four-game visit to New York by the Indians.

In the opener, Babe cracked three doubles, leading the Yanks to a 4–2 win. The teams split the next two games. Game four looked like a must win for the Indians, if they were to stay in the race. For the Yankees, it was the biggest game in the team's history.

Babe added to his legendary clutch hitting, bashing two homers and a double. The Indians never recovered and the Yankees clinched the flag a few days later.

Soon after, on a broiling afternoon in the second game of a meaningless doubleheader with the Yanks holding a 6–0 lead in the eighth, Babe found Yankee manager Miller Huggins in an unusually good mood and wanted to take advantage of it.

Huggins, at just a shade over five feet tall, was certainly not intimidating; in fact, most of the players towered over him. But in their eyes, Huggins managed like a tough but loving father. Even Babe respected and admired him. But unlike the other players, Babe didn't feel the need to approach him cautiously.

Babe grabbed his shoulder and, calling Huggins by the nickname only he dared use, said, "Listen, Flea, it's awfully hot out there today. Wouldn't it be a shame if this heat wore out our pitching staff right before the World Series? Colonel Ruppert might never forgive you."

"Yeah, Babe, you're probably right. What'd you have in mind?" Huggins said.

"Well, skip," Babe went on, trying to be as serious as possible, "you know a lot of these boys already forgot what a star pitcher I was. They don't even remember my World Series records and those duels with ol' Walter Johnson."

"I never forgot, Babe," said Huggins as he rolled his eyes and then squinted at Ruth. "Get to the point. I still gotta manage this crew another two innings and it's too hot to even talk."

"Well," said Babe, his face brightening, "how about I go in and finish the game and show these guys what real control is all about?"

Huggins made a face and shook his head. "I thought we settled this before, when I let you pitch early in the season. You even got the win. Plus, Babe, I always heard how you moaned all those years to Barrow about how you only wanted to hit. Pitching I got. Hitting . . . well, that's your job on the Yankees, Babe. Go sit down and cool off."

But Babe wouldn't take no for an answer and

Babe Bounced Onto the Field.

continued to plead for a chance. Players in the dugout voiced their approval, with Babe's urging behind Huggins's back. As the inning ended and the Yankees prepared to take their positions on the field, Huggins turned to Ruth.

"All right, wise guy," he said. "Get out there and let's see what you've still got. But no relievers for you, Babe. You stay out there till it's over."

Babe was overjoyed and bounced onto the field just as he had when he was a kid at St. Mary's. A cheer went up as the fans realized what was happening.

Much to his, but certainly not Huggins's, surprise, Babe's arm was a little rusty, and he allowed six runs to score. The game was now tied. Sweating rivers in his hot woolen uniform, Babe was sucking in big breaths of heavy, humid air.

Most of the crowd had already gone home to supper. Babe peered into the dugout looking for relief, but Huggins just looked the other way. Hoping to cure his star of ever wanting to take the mound again, Huggins left Babe in.

Then, to Huggins's dismay, Babe settled down, hurled scoreless ball, and recorded still another win, as the Yanks pulled out the game in the eleventh inning.

Babe finished 1921 with what may be the best overall year any hitter has ever had. Including his two just-for-fun pitching wins, Babe stroked a .378 batting average that included 44 doubles, 16 triples and a record 59 home runs (the runner-up, Ken Williams of the St. Louis Browns, had only 24!)

Babe had scored 177 runs and batted in 170! His combination of power and consistency was simply awesome. No one had ever put together back-to-back seasons like Babe had in '20 and '21, and no one has done it since!

New York was in a frenzy as the Yankees

Babe Hurled Scoreless Ball.

opened the World Series against their hometown rivals, the Giants, in a special best five of nine games. All the games would be played at the Polo Grounds, the teams' shared home park.

The Giants were managed by fiery John McGraw and led by third baseman Frankie "The Fordham Flash" Frisch and first baseman George "Highpockets" Kelly, both future Hall of Famers.

McGraw knew Babe well. Years earlier he had tried in vain to purchase Ruth's contract from Baltimore's Jack Dunn, but had lost out to the Red Sox. After that, McGraw, another of the old-timers who favored the "inside game," used to mock Babe's power-hitting style, once commenting that "if he plays every day, the bum will hit into a hundred double plays before he's through."

McGraw didn't like all the attention Babe and the Yanks were now getting. The Giants, who had been in five previous World Series, had "owned" the

BABE RUTH

New York fans since the early 1900s. Now they found themselves sharing not just the same ball-park, but the glory as well. McGraw was determined to stifle Babe in any way he could.

In the first game of the World Series, Babe lined the first pitch he saw for a single, driving in the first run. Carl Mays, with his baffling, almost sidearm delivery, shut out the Giants for a 3–0 Yankee win despite four hits by Frisch. McGraw was beside himself.

In the second game McGraw ordered Giant hurler Art Nehf to be extra careful with Babe at the plate, not to throw anything in the strike zone. After a bad ball base hit, Nehf walked Babe his next three times up.

Relieved at avoiding Babe's awesome power, Nehf wasn't even looking at first after Babe's third base on balls. Then the astonished Giants saw Ruth take off for second, easily stealing the base.

153

Bruised Knee and Infected Elbow

BABE RUTH

A few pitches later he swiped third and Nehf sadly realized that he was in the same trouble as if the Babe had smashed a triple! Yankee pitcher Waite Hoyt held the Giants to two hits and the Yanks won again, 3–0.

With two shutouts and the Yankees leading again in the third game, the crowd began to sense a Yankee rout. But the sleeping Giants awoke with thunder, and led by George Burns's four hits, turned the tables. With an eight-run explosion in the seventh inning, they cruised to a 13–5 victory.

In the Yankee clubhouse, Babe showed Huggins a bruised knee and an infected elbow, which he had scraped up on one of those memorable stolen bases in game two.

Babe had kept the injuries from everyone and had played in extreme pain until he scraped the elbow again by sliding. He had been forced to leave the game early in the eighth frame. In the locker room, the players looked glum; knowing their star would be unable to continue in the Series, their confidence was shattered.

Before the next game, Babe couldn't even take batting practice. He sat in the corner of the dugout holding his arm bent and stiff, not talking to anyone.

But just as the Yankees jumped up to take the field for game four, he suddenly grabbed his glove and announced that he was indeed going to play!

Despite the pain, he managed to hit a solo home run in the bottom of the ninth. But it was not enough; the Giants won the game 4–2.

With Babe's arm still bandaged and his face showing his pain, everyone in the park for game five knew it would be tough for the Babe to get around his massive bat and swing for the fences.

But Babe, ever the pro, again used his incredi-

He Grabbed His Glove!

ble all-around baseball talent and started the winning rally, beating out a perfect bunt down the third base line. He then scored the winning run on a double by the reliable Meusel.

It was a piece of "inside" baseball and the red-faced McGraw couldn't believe his eyes.

When the Babe reached the dugout, he collapsed. He was quickly revived and the crowd went crazy with a wild standing ovation when he trotted to the outfield for the bottom of the inning. Yankee hurler Waite Hoyt allowed just one unearned run as the Yanks edged the Giants 3–1.

Unfortunately, the infected elbow took a turn for the worse. There was fear of blood poisoning or something even more serious.

Babe's heroics were over. Under doctor's orders, he had to watch the next two games, both Yankee losses, from a box seat with Helen at his side.

By the final game Babe was back in uniform.

BABE RUTH

With the Yanks down 1–0 in the bottom of the ninth, Huggins gambled and put Babe in as a pinch hitter. He took a big cut, but managed only a weak grounder. McGraw's Giants were number one in both New York and the world.

Babe Got Restless.

Chapter 11

"The House that Ruth Built"

The elbow healed at last and it wasn't long before the Babe got restless. He convinced Meusel, Mays, and a few other Yanks to join his "Babe Ruth's All-Stars," a team he had formed the year before to barnstorm around the country, playing exhibitions. Babe could double his yearly salary this way—no one could draw a crowd of paying customers like Ruth. They were all set to go when someone got in their way, Judge Kenesaw Mountain Landis.

BABE RUTH

Judge Landis had been appointed baseball commissioner by the team owners after the terrible "Black Sox" scandal of 1919 when a number of Chicago White Sox players, including legendary "Shoeless" Joe Jackson, had accepted money from gamblers to "throw" the Series.

The fix disillusioned the faithful fans and had given the national pastime a bad image—that gamblers and gangsters could decide the outcomes of games. In stepped Landis to watch over baseball and rule the Major Leagues with an iron fist.

Landis was tough and demanded that everything be done his way or no way. His way was strictly by the book. When he heard about Babe's exhibitions, he decided to enforce a rule that had been around since 1911, but rarely, if ever, acted on. The rule forbade players on World Series teams from playing exhibitions after the Series. Meusel and a few other players were getting shaky after

Judge Kenesaw Mountain Landis

Landis's warning, but Babe telephoned the angry commissioner to announce that he was leaving the next day.

"Oh, you are, are you?" shouted the furious Landis. "If you do, it will be the sorriest day you've ever had in baseball!" And he hung up the phone.

Landis turned to some sportswriters who were sitting in his office. "Who does that guy think he is?" he growled. "I'm going to show him who's running this game!"

Landis was intent on enforcing the rule, right or wrong. He hadn't made the rules, he reasoned, but he had been hired to make sure that all ballplayers followed them.

The next day the writers spoke to Babe about Landis's reaction. Babe was angry, too. After all, other players had done the same thing before without any trouble. Why was Landis picking on him?

"Tell him to go jump in a lake," was Babe's reply.

But Landis did have the last word. Meusel and Ruth, the Yankees' two biggest stars, were fined their World Series bonuses and both were suspended for the first six weeks of the 1922 season!

The Yankees meanwhile had gotten even stronger in the off-season. Red Sox owner Harry Frazee had done it again, selling the Yanks his two best pitchers, "Sad" Sam Jones and "Bullet" Joe Bush. When Babe joined them, the Yanks were already in first place.

But the Bambino just couldn't seem to get into his usual groove and was slumping despite an occasional home run. Frustrated and unhappy, Babe easily lost control of his temper.

American League president Ban Johnson had to suspend him four more times that year for arguments with umpires and with heckling fans.

McGraw and His Pitchers

BABE RUTH

Babe soon missed some more time when he was sick with the flu. Yet he still managed a more than respectable 35 homers and 99 RBIs to go with a .315 average. A great year for nearly anyone else, but not for Babe Ruth, and he knew it.

Even without a full-time Babe, the Yankees, led by Joe Bush's 26 wins, won the pennant in a down-to-the-last day battle with the St. Louis Browns. Again they faced the New York Giants in the World Series.

Babe was itching for the Series to begin. He figured it would be a great time to shake off his year of woes. Crafty Giants manager McGraw knew that Ruth would be swinging for the fences, overeager to hit anything to prove to the fans that his ordinary season had been a fluke. McGraw ordered his pitchers to throw only outside curve balls which he hoped Ruth would lunge after anyway.

McGraw was right. The Giants swept the Yankees in the Series and held Babe to a .118 average. Ruth managed only two hits, and no homers.

It was Ruth's greatest disappointment in a disappointing year. To add to the insult, the Giants bragged in the newspapers that they had stolen all the Yankees signs.

There was one thing, however, that brought a ray of sunshine to Babe's life that year. Babe and Helen adopted a baby girl named Dorothy. Even on days where everything else seemed to be going wrong, news of the child's antics brought smiles to the troubled home run king.

During the winter, some New York sportswriters wrote that Babe Ruth had gotten out of shape. They accused him of paying more attention to his wardrobe and his endorsements than to playing baseball. For the first time, the lovable Bambino was being criticized.

At a big dinner, the future mayor of New York,

A Baby Girl Named Dorothy

Jimmy Walker, made a speech in which he accused Babe of disappointing all the kids in New York who idolized him. Walker then looked over to where Babe was seated and asked, "Are you going to keep on letting those little kids down?"

He hit Babe where it hurt the most, because Babe loved kids. He could always just be himself around children. He spent many hours visiting kids in hospitals and orphanages—he had never forgotten the loneliness he felt the day he was sent to St. Mary's.

Babe got up in front of the audience and admitted that he had made many mistakes. Tears rolled down his face as he apologized to his fans, especially the kids, and pledged to return to his farm to work his body back into shape.

"I'm gonna work my head off . . . and maybe some of my stomach too," he said and he promised that the next year would be a great one.

Meanwhile, construction crews were hard at work building a new stadium to hold the crowds that were coming to see Babe Ruth play. McGraw was sick of sharing the Polo Grounds with the Yanks who for the first time had drawn more fans than the Giants.

He secretly hoped that the Yankees would find no place to play and that the fans would just forget about them. But Yankee Stadium, hailed as "the House that Ruth built," was ready for opening day 1923.

It was the grandest stadium ever built. It stood tall and gleaming. No baseball diamond had ever looked more majestic, no grass had ever been greener. Over 74,000 fans, easily the largest crowd ever to see a baseball game, sat elbow to elbow, some kneeling in the aisles.

Thousands more had to be turned away. On everyone's mind was the same question: could Babe

Babe Kept His Promise.

Ruth come back from all his troubles of last year or was he really "over the hill"at age 28?

In the third inning, with two men on, Babe stepped up and delivered just what the fans had come to see, a long home run that beat the dismal Red Sox (now ridiculed as the "Dead Sox") 4–1. It looked like Babe was indeed back, and just as good as before.

The 1923 season was the greatest the Yankees had ever had. They breezed to their third A. L. pennant. Babe Ruth kept his promise and rebounded with a great year capped by his winning the Most Valuable Player Award. Babe slammed American League pitching for a .394 average, belting 41 homers and driving in 130 runs.

Of his 205 hits, an amazing 99 were for extra bases. He walked a record 170 times, testimony to the fear he put in his opponents.

Again the Yanks were matched up against the

Giants in the World Series, and again manager McGraw devised plans to keep the feared Ruth in check.

After losing the first game 5–4 on a two-out, ninth inning inside-the-park home run by Casey Stengel, who danced to the plate even after losing his shoe on the base path, the Yanks rebounded.

In game two, Babe smacked two homers to give pitcher Herb Pennock the win (19-game winner Pennock had been obtained by Barrow in a steal from none other than the Boston Red Sox!) But Babe's longest drive of the day was a clout to deep centerfield which was hauled in on the run by Stengel.

In the third game, a solo homer by Stengel, who disdainfully thumbed his nose as he passed by the Yankee dugout, was all the Giants needed for a 1–0 whitewash. But then, in both of the next two games, the Yankees exploded for eight

Thumbing His Nose

runs and two victories.

Pennock saved game three with some stellar relief work and third baseman Joe Dugan paced the Yank attack in game five with four hits. In game six, Pennock again was aided by a shot by Babe as the Yanks closed out the series with a 6–4 win.

Babe batted a solid .368 in the Series despite McGraw's maneuverings. After the disappointments of 1921 and '22, it was sweet revenge for Babe. After a twenty year wait, the Yankees had finally become champions.

Chapter 12

New York's Bad Boy

Babe had made it all the way back to the top. He was also back to fooling around for photographers and doing almost anything if it seemed like fun. He had a fancy red car that everyone in New York knew was the Bambino's as it was the longest car anyone had ever seen!

Wherever Babe parked it around town, crowds would gather around and wait for him to appear. It got so that he had to change cars every few months just to get some peace.

The Car Was Surrounded.

But if there were any fans he refused to disappoint, it was the kids. One warm afternoon Babe and his family were driving home in his car when they were stopped in traffic. Babe watched as some little boys on a makeshift diamond played ball.

All of a sudden one of the smallest noticed Ruth's car and hollered, "Hey! There's Babe!"

In an instant, Ruth's car was surrounded by kids jumping up and down, calling for their hero to pull over.

"Glad to see you, guys," said Ruth as he stepped out of the car. "You know that's just the way I got started," he added as he absentmindedly picked up the well-worn bat they were using.

"C'mon, Babe, how about taking a few swings with us?" one asked and in chorus they begged and pleaded for him to join the game.

"I don't know, boys, I'm awfully tired today. You know I just played in a doubleheader at Yankee Stadium," he started to explain.

But the instant he saw the looks of disappointment on the boys' faces, he changed his mind. He never could turn down a kid when it had to do with baseball.

Dressed in his fancy street clothes, Ruth grabbed a baseball and stood on the mound. One by one the boys stepped in to take a few swings. Babe threw easily and threw strikes right down the middle.

"Hey, Babe, where'd you ever learn to pitch like that?" asked one little guy who was half the size of his bat.

The Bambino chuckled. He knew these kids were all too young to know anything about his great pitching days. "Oh, a guy I once knew named Matthias showed me a few tricks when I was on the Red Sox quite a few years ago," said Babe, smiling.

Then Babe switched sides and hit some balls

Everything from Cereal to Candy

around the field, mostly easy ones that the kids could catch.

"Aw, Babe, let's see some real power," one said, and Babe promptly hit a few long drives that left the kids open-mouthed and satisfied.

After autographing a few scraps of paper, Babe suddenly heard the car horn beep. He had left his wife and daughter sitting in the car for nearly an hour when he had intended to be gone only about ten minutes!

Ruth dusted himself off, waved goodbye, and roared away in his sleek automobile. It was an hour that none of those kids would ever forget!

Babe became so well known that if his big smiling face was on a product, people bought it—everything from cereal and candy to wristwatches and even boxes of underwear!

There were books and magazines written about him, and he even went to Hollywood to make movies. In the winter, he went on a theater tour; onstage, he swung at baseballs hung on string and talked about his record home runs.

One time he swung so hard he lost his balance and fell off the stage, crashing into the orchestra. When he jumped up and announced that he was all right, the audience roared with laughter and applause—America loved every minute of George Herman Ruth.

Unlike today's players, the Babe never refused an autograph to anyone, and he didn't charge for them either. He never disappointed any of his fans, no matter where he was or what he was doing.

After spring training, the Yankees would head back up north by train, stopping off at places where there was no Major League baseball, to play their final exhibitions. Telegraph operators all along the way would signal the small towns, telling them what train Babe Ruth would be on.

Babe Never Refused an Autograph.

BABE RUTH

Hundreds, sometimes even thousands of people, some of whom had traveled by horse and buggy for a day or more and many of whom had never even seen a baseball game, would wait at the stations until the train came by. If they were lucky, the train would stop for a minute and Babe, dressed in his famous camel hair coat and cap, would come out and say hello.

On the train, Babe held court with reporters and ran card games. He'd treat everyone to fried chicken, ribs and ice cream which he would buy along the way.

He was always generous with his money. When the team stayed in a town overnight, Babe was sure to know the owner of the best restaurant and the best hotel and where to get the best of everything else. The red carpet was always rolled out for the Bambino and his friends wherever they went. The champion Yankees were having a ball.

BABE RUTH

Babe had another super year in 1924, winning the batting title with a .378 average. He smacked 46 homers with 121 RBIs and led the league in walks and runs. He just missed winning the Triple Crown by a few RBIs.

But this Yankee team was getting older and more injury-prone. They began to slip a little. Late in the season a well-balanced Washington Senator team overtook them. This was especially odd because Washington was not a top team. In fact there was a saying about the team that went "Washington—first in war, first in peace, and last in the American League."

But led by Ruth's old pitching rival, the great Walter Johnson, the Senators took the pennant by two games, stopping the Yankee streak at three.

The next spring, Babe showed up at spring training out-of-shape and suffering from a case of the flu which he seemed to get every year about this

The Great Walter Johnson

time.

On the trip back home, Babe ate a dozen hot dogs and washed them down with a gallon of soda pop. He collapsed on the train and had to be hospitalized. The newspaper headlines called it "The Bellyache Heard Round the World." Further weakened by an operation, Babe missed the 1925 opening game.

When he returned to the team, Babe didn't give up his carefree ways. He still liked to eat meals that would kill an elephant and stay out late at night. He used to laugh and say that Huggins had a rule that he had to be in the hotel by one o'clock, but that Huggins never said if that was A.M. or P.M.

Soon the Yankees fell to seventh place. Huggins was fed up with the behavior of his star, who was having his worst season ever. Huggins also felt that Babe was setting a bad example for the other players.

BABE RUTH

One afternoon, the Babe arrived at the ballpark where the Yanks were playing and was about to change into his uniform.

"Don't bother hanging up that jacket, Babe," said Huggins, from a chair in a corner of the locker room. "You don't have to bother dressing today. You're not helping the club any and we don't need you. I'm fining and suspending you. You can go back upstairs, and my secretary will give you your ticket so you can go back to New York."

Babe turned around and glared at Huggins. He carefully put his jacket back on and then started to yell at Huggins, calling him every name he could think of.

Huggins stood his ground, silently listening. But when Babe stopped for breath, Huggins spoke again.

"You know, Babe, someday you'll change your mind and thank me for what I'm doing now. But

Reporters Found the Furious Babe.

until you apologize to me and your teammates and straighten yourself out, you're never going to play another game for the New York Yankees."

With that, Huggins turned and left to meet the other players.

By that evening, news of the suspension was everywhere. Reporters found the furious Babe and asked for his comment.

"I can't understand it," snorted Babe. "I'm in as good condition as I've ever been. He's just trying to blame me for the poor shape the team's in when everybody knows it's his fault," he shouted as he got angrier and angrier. "Well, boys, it's either him or me. If they want to keep him as manager, they can just go get another right fielder, and that's that!"

Babe was sure that team owner Ruppert would side with him. It was the Bambino who put all the fans in those seats at Yankee Stadium, not the little manager, he reasoned. And that fine of $5000—Babe moaned that murderers had gotten off for less!

But back in his office in New York, Colonel Ruppert, hearing about Babe's demand, had a surprising reply for his star.

"Tell Mr. Ruth that I back my manager a hundred percent! The fine sticks, and the suspension stays in effect as long as Huggins says it does," insisted the exasperated owner. "And you can tell Ruth one more thing," Ruppert continued. "Tell him that Miller Huggins is my manager as long as he wants to be."

By the next day, as had happened after his clashes with Ed Barrow, Babe softened. "Aw, I guess I was a little rash," he told reporters. "What I really meant was that I couldn't do my best playing for him until we straighten things out between us. Hey, New York is my town. I don't want to play

"I Back My Manager 100%!"

anywhere else!"

Huggins and Ruppert let Babe stew for a week or so before they had a meeting. The fine and the suspension stuck. Babe, like a little boy who had been punished by his parents, solemnly came back and sincerely apologized to everyone. By September he was back in uniform, but it was too late for the Yanks, who were only kept out of last place by the even more miserable Red Sox.

It was a sorry year for Babe, who finished 1925 with a .290 average and only 25 home runs. Bob Meusel won the home run title with 33 and led the league in RBIs, too. The Bambino's shadow didn't seem so big all of a sudden. In the newspapers and on the streets, the talk was that Babe Ruth at age 31 was finally through.

Chapter 13

On and Off the Field

"I'm going to make good all over again," said Babe Ruth after the 1925 season. He was ashamed of the sudden Yankee collapse, but knew in his heart he had a lot of baseball left in him. Every day that winter, he worked hard in the gym.

By spring training, muscle had replaced the previous year's fat. The Babe was ready to show the world that he still was the one and only "Sultan of Swat."

During the off-season Barrow had made some

He Worked Hard in the Gym.

changes. Added to the solid core of Ruth, Meusel, and Dugan were a number of promising young players.

Tony Lazzeri, a rookie, was at second. Mark Koenig, in his second year, took over at short. Earl Combs joined the outfield in center, and an unproven first baseman named Lou Gehrig finally got his chance to play full time.

Of this group, only Koenig and Dugan would fail to make the Hall of Fame. The fine pitching staff was led by ace control artist Pennock, veteran Hoyt, and newcomer Urban Shocker.

The "new" Yankees edged out Tris Speaker's Cleveland Indians for the '26 pennant and Babe contributed mightily. He batted .372 and led the league in homers with 47 (Al Simmons of the Athletics was second with a mere 19), 145 RBIs, and 139 runs, just missing the Triple Crown.

But the young Yankees were not quite ready for

the role of champions, as the Yankees lost to the St. Louis Cardinals four games to three in the World Series.

The Cardinal hero was forty-year-old pitcher Grover Cleveland Alexander, whom Ruth had seen in the 1915 Series when Alexander was in his prime. "Alexander The Great," suffering from epileptic seizures and personal problems, remarkably won games two and six.

One of the most heartwarming stories about Babe Ruth came in the middle of the Series, and a young fan was the co-star of the day. Eleven-year-old Johnny Sylvester lay in a hospital bed gravely injured from a fall. The players happened to hear about Johnny, who was a big baseball fan and, before game four, sent him a baseball that had been signed by the stars of both the Cards and the Yanks.

In the package, Babe included a personal note to Johnny. In it he urged Johnny to try hard to get

Gravely Injured from a Fall

well. Ruth also promised the young fan that he would hit a homer just for him.

Johnny listened to the game on the radio and was quite surprised when Babe didn't exactly keep his promise. Instead of just one, Ruth walloped a Series record three homers that day, leading the Yankees to a 10–5 victory.

After the Series was over, Babe paid Johnny a visit in the hospital. Thanks to Babe Ruth, Johnny recovered faster than any of his doctors ever thought he would.

The Cards and Yanks split games five and six. In the seventh and deciding game Babe homered again, but the Yanks still trailed 3–2.

Alexander, still woozy from the celebration for his victorious game six, was unexpectedly called upon in relief. He saved the win by striking out Tony Lazzeri with the bases loaded in the seventh and blanked the Yanks the rest of the way for a save.

BABE RUTH

Babe was blamed for one of the few bonehead plays he ever made when, standing on first with two out in the ninth inning, he suddenly took off trying to steal second. The throw nailed him easily for the final out of the Series before a stunned Yankee Stadium crowd.

The 1927 Yankees have been picked by most baseball experts as the greatest team of all time. The awesome lineup, nicknamed "Murderer's Row," propelled the team to a record 110 victories.

Everyone in the lineup contributed. Combs, an outstanding leadoff man with a gold glove, batted .356. The always dependable Meusel hit .337 and knocked home 103 runs. Lazzeri came into his own, driving in 102 runs with a .309 average.

But the real excitement that year was not the pennant race, which was already decided by May, but the home run contest between two of the game's greatest sluggers, Babe and Lou Gehrig. They

The Bambino Lunged Forward.

matched each other clout for clout until late August when Babe began to pull away.

Ruth was determined to set a new home run record. By the next to the last game of the season, Ruth's total stood at 59. The Yanks faced pitcher Tom Zachary of the Washington Senators.

Zachary knew that the Babe was hot—he had smacked three homers in his last three games. Zachary became the object of the booing fans when he walked Babe on four terrible pitches first time up. The next two times Babe connected, but only for singles.

With the score tied 2–2 in the eighth, Ruth faced Zachary for the final time. Zachary fired a curve ball, high and straight at Babe, a pitch that was nearly impossible to hit. Zachary wanted to back him off the plate, but instead, the Bambino lunged forward for the ball and whacked it.

The fly ball steered along the right field line

going deeper and deeper. Then it dropped into the right-field stands, just inches fair. Zachary ran towards the plate screaming, "Foul, Foul!" to the ump, but it was no use. Babe had his record homer!

During the celebration, Ruth could be heard to say, "Sixty! Count 'em—sixty! Let's see some other son-of-a-gun match that!" Along with his sixty dingers, the Babe finished the season with a .356 average, knocking in 164 runs and scoring 158!

Teammate Gehrig, although out–dueled in the home-run derby, matched Babe's .356 mark and won the RBI crown with 175 to go with his 47 homers.

During batting practice before game one of the World Series, the awestruck Pittsburgh Pirates watched "Murderer's Row" belt one ball after another out of the park. It's said that Gehrig hit ten out in a row, and then Ruth hit twelve!

One by one the Pirates left the field muttering to themselves. "They're beaten already," commented

Gehrig Batted Behind Babe.

BABE RUTH

Dodger manager Wilbert Robinson to some onlookers who watched the awesome display. New York swept the Pirates in the Series. Ruth batted .400 with two homers in the wipeout.

With the same lineup, the Yankees won the 1928 pennant. Gehrig batted fourth behind the Babe, giving the Yanks the most devastating pair of power-hitters ever to take the diamond. The duo led the Yankees against the Cardinals once again in the World Series.

This time there was no magic left in Alexander's arm, nor any punch in the St. Louis bats, as the Cards were swept in four games. That made eight winning World Series games in a row for the Yanks.

Babe batted a whopping .625, a Series record, and put on a show, socking three homers in game four. Gehrig blasted four homers to go with his .545 series average.

BABE RUTH

During these glory years, Helen had grown to dislike the whirlwind New York life. She preferred to remain in Boston or at the Ruth farm.

One bitterly cold night in January, firemen responded to a fire at a Boston apartment. There they found the body of poor Helen, who had died in the terrible flames. The authorities got hold of Babe and gave him the bad news.

For days, Ruth paced his hotel room floor; he couldn't eat or sleep. Helen was laid to rest, and Babe realized that for his and little Dorothy's sake, he had to get on with his life.

Later Babe married Claire Hodgsen, an actress he had known for many years. She had a young daughter and wanted to have a whole family again as much as Babe did. Claire was always known as the one who finally kept Babe in line.

In 1929, despite the addition of Hall of Fame catcher Bill Dickey, the team started slipping. Pen-

Many Players Broke Down and Cried.

nock, Hoyt and even Meusel began to show their age. The Philadelphia Athletics, led by rising stars like Al Simmons and the "new Babe Ruth," Jimmy Foxx, were the new American League champs.

As the Yanks played out September in Fenway Park, manager Huggins lay ill in the hospital. Everyone thought the frail "Flea" was just tired from the stress of the long season. He'd be back with them soon enough, the players knew. But during the game, Barrow appeared in the dugout and told the team that Huggins had passed away.

The news really shook up everyone, including the sentimental Babe, who felt nearly as bad as when Big George had passed away. Many of the players broke down and cried. The Yankees finished the game and won. They continued to play well for the last few games, like the true professionals that Huggins had taught them to be.

Huggins was replaced in 1930 by Bob Shawkey,

but the Yanks finished in third place. Babe banged out 49 homers, 153 RBIs and a .359 average, but with injuries and retirements, the pitching staff and "Murderer's Row" were not quite what they had been.

Joe McCarthy succeeded Shawkey as manager. Actually Babe had hoped that he would be named player-manager. He had seen both Speaker and Cobb do the same near the end of their careers. But Barrow laughed and wouldn't even consider it. After all, he explained, Ruth could barely take care of himself and follow rules. How would he ever be able to manage thirty stubborn ballplayers? Babe was insulted and would always resent McCarthy, but he kept it quiet.

McCarthy was the best thing that could happen to the fading Bronx Bombers. He was driven to win and wanted no less than to destroy the opponent every time out. He was tough and enforced disci-

Babe Banged Out 49 Homers.

pline. He drilled his squad in fundamentals, veterans and rookies alike. Before he was through, many would regard him as the greatest manager ever.

Together, Barrow and McCarthy set out to rebuild the franchise. In 1931, the Yankees moved up in the standings, finishing second. Babe had his usual great year, hitting .373 and tying Gehrig for the home run lead with 49. With Ruth frequently on base ahead of him, Gehrig set a record with 184 RBIs that still stands today.

As baseball's greatest attraction for many years, Babe was paid far more than anyone else. His colossal $80,000 salary was even more than President Hoover made. When asked about that, Babe jokingly replied, "Why not! I had a better year than he did!"

In 1932, the Yankees came all the way back, winning 107 games. Lefty Gomez and Red Ruffing anchored a fine pitching staff. For the first time, though, the 38-year-old Babe showed his age. He was noticeably slower, and for the first time since 1925 he lost the home-run title to the A's Jimmy Foxx, hitting only 41 to go with his .341 average.

The Yanks faced the Chicago Cubs in a classic World Series. There was bad blood between the teams. Joe McCarthy had once been fired by the Cubs, the owner calling him a loser. Also, ex-Yankee Mark Koenig at the end of his career was brought in by the Cubs to replace their injured shortstop. Koenig hit over .350 and was spectacular in the field. He was a major reason the Cubs won the pennant.

But the greedy Cubs players decided before the Series to vote Koenig only a half-share of their Series bonus money. That outraged the Yankees; Koenig still had lots of friends on the team. Babe didn't hold back, railing to reporters about the "cheap bums" those Cubs were.

Both Benches Hurled Insults and Each Other.

BABE RUTH

The Yankees won the first two games, played at the Stadium. Feelings were bitter—both benches hurled insults at each other throughout the games. When the scene shifted to Chicago's Wrigley Field, things grew worse. On the way into the hotel Babe and Claire were spat upon, and thousands of onlookers cursed the Yankee players.

In the third game, the score was tied in the fifth inning 4–4. Babe had already hit a two-run homer in the first inning. Now Babe waited to face Cub pitcher Charlie Root. Some fruit was thrown from the stands as Babe kneeled in the on-deck circle. The Cubs, some of them on the top step of the dugout, were beside themselves.

"Hey, you fat pig, you're all washed up!" one screamed, the veins bulging from his neck. Another jumped up and down giving Ruth the choke sign, acting like he was strangling him. 50,000 fans were screaming taunts at Babe as he stepped in.

BABE RUTH

Babe looked around and smiled. Root went into his windup and fired a strike that Babe hardly even looked at. Babe held up one finger. "That's one," he said. Again Root delivered another strike. "That's two," Babe smiled, looking over at the Cubbies. He had not even moved his bat yet.

Now the crowd was even louder, but Babe remained calm and cool. He even looked like he was enjoying being in this pressure cooker. Ruth stepped back and grabbed a handful of dirt, the bat held loosely in his hand.

The Cubs were calling him all sorts of names. Some had even moved out of the dugout onto the field.

As he was rubbing his hands, Babe looked directly into the Cub dugout. He waved the players back to sit down and with a smile, raised two fingers and then pointed out to the center field fence.

Babe slowly set himself in the batter's box. He

Babe Pointed to the Center Field Fence.

looked down at Cub catcher Gabby Hartnett and said, "You know, kid, it only takes one to hit it. If that bum throws another one in here, I'm gonna hit it over the fence." Then Babe looked at out Root and screamed, "I'm gonna knock the next one right down your throat!"

Root snarled, reared back and threw a fastball right above the knees. Babe uncoiled that beautiful swing of his and with the crack of the bat, all eyes looked to the outfield.

Like a rifle shot, the ball kept traveling, clear out of the ballpark and smack into a tree. It was the longest homer ever in Wrigley Field! The Bambino had called his shot!

As he rounded third he was bombarded with fruit. He smiled and thought to himself, *why, you lucky bum.*

Lou Gehrig followed the blast with another homer (Lou also had two in the game) that put the Cubs away for good. The Yankees won the fourth game for a sweep of this bitter World Series.

The year 1932 marked Babe's final World series appearance. What a way to finish, with his 15th Series home run!

Letting the Legend Grow

Chapter 14

Calling the Shots

To his dying day, Charlie Root and many of the other Cubs insisted that Ruth did not point to the outfield before he delivered his massive home run. Root especially couldn't stand having been shown up by baseball's greatest showman. But many of the Yankee players insisted that the legendary story was indeed true. Babe himself would never settle the argument, preferring instead to allow the legend to grow on its own.

But it should come as no surprise to anyone

that Ruth did call his shot; after all, he had done it before. He had delivered on his promise to young Johnny Sylvester who lay ill in the hospital when he smashed that homer in the 1926 World Series against the Cardinals. And there were other memorable occasions when Ruth seemed to hit one out on sheer willpower, something that few other baseball players have ever been able to do, no matter how talented they were. One of the best happened in Boston when Babe was playing against the Red Sox.

Whenever the Yankees visited Boston they could be sure that the near-empty Fenway Park would be ringing with the taunts of one particular fan. This man made it his business to call Ruth every name in the book. Ever since Babe's departure from the Sox, the team had been in sorry straits, and the Beantown fans had little to cheer for.

This one fan in particular seemed to blame Babe for the decline of the once-proud Boston club.

One Particular Fan

In a way he was right, because the franchise had never been the same since Ruth had been sold to the Yankees.

But most other fans realized that the sale was not Ruth's idea, but that of former team owner Harry Frazee. Nonetheless, when the Yanks came to town, this disgruntled Red Sox fan attended every game and he delighted in heaping abuse on Ruth and his teammates.

With the last place Red Sox drawing only a handful of fans to each game, his voice always seemed to be louder than anything else as it echoed through the stands. Babe and his teammates usually laughed off the man's many catcalls, but one day his comments were even nastier than ever.

The fan had crept down behind the Yankee dugout and unleashed a torrent of insults at Ruth. Babe pretty much ignored the fellow until he heard some terrible things being said about his wife and family.

"Why, I ought to go out and wring that guy's neck," muttered Ruth as he jumped off the bench and began to pace in the dugout.

He grew more agitated with each insult and each step.

"I can take all the yapping about my weight and all," cautioned the now steaming Babe. "But getting on my family is way out of line. Watch me go bust this guy in the nose, fellas, and don't anyone try and hold me back."

In a flash, Babe was on the top step of the dugout, peering into the box seats and trying to pinpoint the irritating voice that continued the nasty stream of comments.

"Hold on, Babe," shouted one of the Yankees. "We can't afford to have you suspended...it's too close to the World Series and we're gonna need you on the field. Besides, you're on deck!"

Babe Bowed Before Disappearing.

Ruth noticed that he was indeed due up next. He selected his bat from the rack and knelt in the on-deck circle, studying the pitcher and trying to ignore for the moment the continuing abuse hurled by the fan.

A pitch or two later Ruth stepped up to the plate. As he settled in, he turned and stared right at his tormentor. After taking a look at the first pitch, he stepped back and pointed to the right field stands.

On the next pitch Babe launched a screaming line drive that quickly disappeared over the fence for a home run. Amidst an eerie silence, Babe trotted around the bases, head down until he crossed the plate. He then stopped and turned to the seat where the fan sat suddenly speechless. Then Babe bowed before disappearing into the dugout.

Another of Babe's legendary "called shots" took place as the Yankees were finishing out a homestand. Babe noticed that the Yankees' traveling secretary was nervously wringing his hands and glancing at his watch.

"What's the matter?" Babe shouted over to the little man who was beside himself with worry. "You look like a wreck."

"I am, Babe, I am," blurted the secretary as he again glanced at his watch.

The secretary's job was to make sure that the team and all its equipment got to the train station on time. This particular game had already gone on longer than usual and was still tied in the late innings. Even worse, the opposing pitcher seemed to have the Yankees' number that day as he had held them in check since early in the game. If the game went into extras, the team might miss their train and not reach their destination in time for the next day's contest.

"I just know that we're going to miss our train," the secretary explained to Ruth. "It's getting late.

"You Look Like a Wreck."

You know Barrow holds me responsible for these things...it could even mean my job." The man looked near tears.

"Don't worry. We'll make that train," said Ruth with a twinkle in his eye. "I can just about guarantee it."

The secretary couldn't help but wonder how Ruth could make such an outlandish promise. The Yankee bats looked cold and even Babe had looked bad, striking out in his last at-bat.

As the Yankees came to bat in the next inning, time was running out. The secretary was beside himself, reviewing railroad schedules and trying to figure out how he would transport the team if they missed the train.

Ruth looked over, bat in hand, and caught the man's attention.

"Go ahead and get ready. We're going to make that train," Ruth informed him.

The secretary began to walk down the tunnel that led from the dugout to the locker room shaking his head. He knew that if the game went into extra innings all was lost.

Suddenly he heard the crack of bat meeting baseball, followed by a loud roar from the fans. As he turned in surprise, he was greeted by a mob of Yankee players rushing to the clubhouse. They looked jubilant as they pushed by.

"What happened?" asked the secretary as he stopped one of the players.

"Babe just creamed one...the game's over!" was the reply as the player rushed off. The secretary looked up and there was Ruth talking excitedly to a reporter as he made his way along. Babe caught sight of the traveling secretary and gave him a wink.

"What are you doing standing around here?" Ruth shouted at him. "We've got a train to catch!"

Babe Pitched His Final Game.

Chapter 15

Final Inning

No athlete can go on forever. Babe Ruth sported a big belly now and couldn't run much. He hit only .301 in 1933 with 34 homers. But he still had a few baseball thrills left in him.

Late in the season in '33, Babe pitched his final game. For five innings he held the Red Sox scoreless, and like a storybook hero, got to the plate and stroked a game-winning homer.

The first ever All-Star game was held in 1933. The Babe's third inning homer, with one on, gave the American League a victory.

In 1934 Babe played his final year with the Yankees. Batting only .288 with 22 homers, he told everyone that he would return the next year only if he could manage. Barrow still refused, slamming the door in the face of the man who had made the Yankees the most famous team in sports history.

For the 1935 season, Babe joined the Boston Braves as a playing assistant manager. He was promised that he would be manager by the next year.

But the Braves' owner had lied. He only wanted Ruth because fans would still pay to see him even if he was just coaching. His batting eye gone for good, Ruth struggled at the plate, hitting only .188.

He decided to retire, but had one last Babe Ruth kind of day. In Pittsburgh, Babe somehow turned back the clock, smashing three long homers in succession. The last one, number 714 of his

Babe Turned Back the Clock.

career, went clear over the roof of Forbes Field—the first time it had ever been done. It was the last hit of his career.

The years passed and the Babe waited for offers to get back into baseball, but the call never came.

Babe's health took a turn for the worse. He knew he was dying.

April 27th, 1947 was proclaimed Babe Ruth Day, and he appeared before 60,000 fans at Yankee Stadium. It was a terribly sad day. The Bambino stooped, frail and in pain. The body that had powered the Sultan of Swat was gone, yet it was unmistakably Babe before the microphone.

His voice was a hoarse whisper as he began to speak. "The only real game in the world, I think, is baseball," he said. He spoke mostly about kids and baseball that afternoon. When he was done, he thanked everybody, waved, and walked ever so slowly from the sunlit Yankee Stadium field.

BABE RUTH

The crowd, quiet for a moment, tears welling in their eyes, stood and gave Babe his final cheer. A few months later, he was gone. The sun had set on an era.

For all those years, all those records—right up to the day he turned young for a moment and hit those last three home runs—Babe Ruth had lived and played the game of baseball with the same enthusiasm and joy as when he fielded that first grounder off the bat of Brother Matthias.

It's true that some of Babe's records have been broken. In 1961, Yankee Roger Maris topped Ruth's single season home run mark with 61, but without taking anything away from Maris, it should be noted that he played in ten more games that year than Babe Ruth did when he hit 60.

Everybody knows that all-time great Hank Aaron hit 755 career home runs, eclipsing Babe's

The Greatest Player of All Times

mark of 714. But let's not forget that Babe played in 795 less games than "Hammerin' Hank" did. That's the equivalent of nearly five extra seasons!

A check of the record books finds that Babe retired with a .342 lifetime batting average, the 10th best ever. He was second to Aaron in RBIs, second to Cobb in runs, and first in bases on balls with an astounding 2,056 in his career. Ruth led the league in home runs twelve times.

His single season records for slugging percentage, runs, total bases, walks, and extra base hits still stand to this day.

The baseball fan today can remember Babe Ruth as the tough but kindhearted kid from St. Mary's who not only learned to play the game, but went on to become the greatest baseball player of all time.